The books which help you
most are those which
make you think the most.
The hardest way of learning
is by easy reading:
but a great book that comes
from a great thinker—
it is a ship of thought, deep
freighted with truth and
with beauty.

—Theodore Parker

The People
You Meet
&
The Books
You Read

Books by Charles E. Jones

Life Is Tremendous
Motivational Classics
The Books You Read – Professional Edition
The Books You Read – Devotional Edition
The Books You Read – Historical Edition

You are the same today
as you will be five years from now
except for two things—

The
People You Meet and
THE BOOKS
You Read

edited by
Charles E. Jones

Foreword by
Og Mandino

Published by
Executive Books
P.O. Box 1044, Harrisburg PA 17108

To Gloria

Foreword

by Og Mandino, CPAE

Several years ago, while on tour to promote one of my books, I was asked a question by a television talk show host that I hadn't heard before. After he had introduced me and I had taken my seat, he held up a copy of my latest book and asked, "Og, what will this book do for me?"

I pondered for several moments and then replied, "It might not do anything for you. It's just a book . . . composed of a little ink, some wood pulp, and glue. If you take that book home tonight and read it expecting that your world will change for the better as soon as you finish, then you might as well have taken the money you spent on the book and thrown it away instead."

Unlike the aspirin, that one can take and then wait passively for the headache to disappear, a good book will do nothing for you if it is read with your eyes open but your mind and heart closed. Especially does this apply to books in the self-help and inspirational field. You are wasting your time and your money exploring this great area of literature unless you apply yourself differently when reading these classics than you would some light piece of adventure or romance or even the comic strips.

Let's say you have a problem and you recognize that you do. For example, you know that you just don't have a very high opinion of yourself and this gnawing self-doubt about your abilities is holding you back in both your personal and business life. Someone, a friend perhaps, also recognizing your problem, has suggested that you get yourself a copy of Maxwell Maltz's *Psycho-Cybernetics*. Now you are in your living room, sitting comfortably in your favorite chair, holding that great classic. Before you begin, you must convince yourself of one important fact . . . that Dr. Maltz knows a great deal more about rebuilding your self-image than you do. And, since your present way of life has not enjoyed much success, you are going to take the advice of this acknowledged expert and begin applying it to your life.

Now begin reading . . . with an open mind and a pen or pencil in your hand. Whenever you come upon a suggestion or an idea that you think might be beneficial to you, underline it. Read the entire book in this manner . . . and don't hurry. Speed reading may be great if you're trying to hurry through some report for a meeting in an hour but it won't do anything for you if you are trying to soak in advice that will make a permanent change in your life.

When you have finished with the book, put it aside for a few days. Then, pick it up and read it again. Yes, again. Nobody said this would be easy. On the second reading, you will be pleasantly surprised to note how much you missed on your first read-through. On this second trip you might want to limit yourself to a chapter a day. If it takes twenty days, so what? Isn't this extra effort worth it if you come out of the experience being a better salesperson, sales manager, coach, parent . . . or human being?

Many years ago, when I was just about as complete a failure as one can become, I began to spend a good deal of time in libraries, looking for some answers. Where had I gone wrong? How could I possibly have fouled up my life so badly? And, was it too late for me . . . a thirty-five year old wanderer with only a high school education?

I found all the answers I needed in that golden vein of ore that every library has, that special shelf of books devoted to success, how to achieve it, and how to hold on to it after one attains it. My counselors were some of the wisest people who have ever lived . . . people like Elbert Hubbard, Norman Vincent Peale, W. Clement Stone, Napoleon Hill, Dale Carnegie, Maxwell Maltz, Louis Binstock and Dorothea Brande. The advice from their books helped to change my life.

I read their words with an open mind and a burning desire to change . . . and I had nothing to lose by accepting their principles and applying them to a life that had been wasted up to that time. I owe them so very much and in every book I write I am still trying to repay my debt.

This marvelous book that you are now holding is unique . . . a shopping list, really, to guide you to the very best work that man and woman has written dealing with many areas of your life. Search these pages carefully and I am certain that you will discover exactly the book or books that will help you to deal with your specific problem, whatever it may be. Just think of the time alone that this precious reference will save you in your personal search for the answers you need in order to reach your full potential.

We all need help. There is no such thing as a self-made man or woman. Charles "Tremendous" Jones has performed a miracle through this book. He has created a vehicle, a channel if you will, that will lead you to the perfect specialist that can cure whatever is preventing you from making the progress you deserve. You are a miracle, God's greatest miracle, and now you have a guide that will lead you to the answers you need and prove to yourself, as well as others, how great you really are. Happy hunting, good reading, and joyful living!

Contents

Great Thoughts On Books

A Book I Would Like To Share

Cooper, Kenneth	Tough Times Never Last, But Tough People Do 69
Cousins, Norman	Autobiography of Lincoln Steffens 70
Crowley, Mary	The Tyranny of the Urgent 71
Curry, Bill	Exodus 72

College Football Coaches 73

Paterno, Joe	The Royal Road to Romance
Akers, Fred	Tough Times Never Last, But Tough People Do
Royal, Darrell	Leaves of Gold
Curcio, John	The Will to Manage 74
Danforth, William	The Art of Thinking 75
Danner, R. L.	The One Minute Manager 76
DeBerry, Fisher	Tough Times Never Last, But Tough People Do 77
DeVos, Rich	How to Win Friends & Influence People 78

CEOs 79

O'Connor, James	In Search of Excellence
Charatan-Berger, D.	Getting to Yes
Rolland, Ian	Profiles in Courage
Oreffice, Paul	Atlas Shrugged
Dixon, Greg	Common Sense 80

Great Americans

Patrick Henry-Daniel Webster 81	
Donahue, Terry	Growing Strong in the Seasons of Life 82
Dooley, Vincent	Lee, The Last Years 83

Football 84

Staubach, Roger	The Lou Gehrig Story
Reeves, Dan	Bodyguard of Lies
Emanuel, Frank	The Hairy Ape
Douglass, Merrill	Mere Christianity 85
Dowling, John	Plays of William Shakespeare 86
Eckerman, Arthur	The Discoverers 87
Edmondson, Vern	That Man Is You 88
Eklund, Coy	As a Man Thinketh 89
Etchison, Michael	Beyond Survival 90
Faust, Gerry	The Greatest Miracle in the World 91
Feinerman, Aaron	Sayings of the Fathers 92
Furland, Richard	The Elements of Style 93

CEOs 94

Masland, Frank Jr.	Anthology of Joseph Conrad
O'Neill, Michael	Whale of a Territory
Clay, Orson	As a Man Thinketh
Gardner, John	Montaigne's Essays 95
Rousseau-Hillis	Thoughts About Education 96

The Book

Wooden, John   Magnificent Obsession

Thomas Merton and Books 192

Michaud, Rudolph   Passages 193

Malcolm Muggeridge and Books 194

Murchison, William   Life of Johnson 195
Murphey, Bob   Will Rogers, The Man and His Times 196
Myers, Gordon   Plain Speaking 197
Nash, E. William   Surprised by Joy 198
O'Reilly, A. J. F.   The Great Marlborough & His Duchess 199
Osborne, Tom   The Road Less Traveled 200

CEOs 201

Ferguson, James   The Fountainhead
Flanagan, Robert   Just and Unjust Ways
Barker, Hugh   Man's Search for Meaning
Moore, Dan   Politics: Who Gets What, When & How

Parker, Jim   Magic of Thinking Big 202

George Patton and Books 203

Great Americans 204
Ulysses S. Grant
Robert E. Lee

Peale, Norman Vincent   The Success System That Never Fails 205

William Penn The Scholar 206

Petersen, J. Allan   Beyond Success and Failure 207

Vietnam POWs 208

Plumb, Charles   The Right Stuff
Gaither, Ralph   Believed to be Alive
Mulligan, James   My Beloved My Friend
Davis, Ed   Odyssey

Executives 209

Powell, Howard   A Business and Its Beliefs
McFarland, Kenneth   Human Action

Putnam, Ellen   The Letters of T. E. Lawrence 211
Rawley, John   Autobiography of Benjamin Franklin 212
Rowell, L. J. "Bud"   Reminiscences 213
Rush, Ed   Three Steps Forward, Two Steps Back 214
Rusher, William   Road to Serfdom 215

Heroes: Carl Sandburg and Bernard Baruch 216

Schuller, Robert   Ride the Wild Horses 217
Simon, William   Scaramouche 218
Smith, Fred   The Richest Man in Babylon 219
Smock, Raymond   United States Constitution 220
Sportelli, Louis   Life Is Tremendous 221
Stenger, Walter   The Knowledge of the Holy 222

Great Thoughts on Reading

Introduction

Every good thought, every good thing that has happened in my life is related directly or indirectly to a book. That should explain my motivation for this book. If I lived a million years, I could not repay the debt of gratitude I feel for those who invested their lives in writing and the many who thought enough of me to give me a book.

My management training began with a Sunday School class of young boys in 1950. My dear friend, Willard Niesen, gave me a book by Donald Grey Barnhouse. That book helped me enough that the boys were able to give me time to learn to teach.

My early business experience was one failure and discouragement after another. My boss, Bill Meckley, gave me a book by Paul Speicher that fueled my hopes and dreams. One line that I've never forgotten: "An attitude of gratitude flavors everything you do." I discovered through books that if you keep working and are thankful, success is inevitable.

Each of my children have been a blessing and a challenge. Only through the books we read together, that I gave them, or they discovered, did we weather the storms and become closer rather than drift further apart. Now I'm experiencing the same joy of closeness with my grandchildren through book reading and memorizing incentives.

It was through a severe physical crisis that lasted several months that I began to read with my heart and not just my mind. No drugs could have provided the 'high' of realizing all those wonderful truths that lay dormant in me awaiting words to frame the thoughts so I could think, share, and experience them.

Through books even success took on a different meaning when after exceeding all my financial dreams and pushing forty, I suddenly lost everything. The following years were agonizing, humiliating and frustrating. But because of books, those years became the most wonderful of my life. Books helped me to laugh at heartaches, concentrate on the essential, and be thankful in everything. Authors, Oswald Chambers and Watchman Nee, became my closest friends even though I had never met either one.

And finally my marriage. How wonderful it would be if all our courtship dreams would turn into reality following the marriage. Fortunately for Gloria and me, we were totally committed to each other, but we were still in different worlds. Books changed that too. One of my favorite authors is A. W. Tozer. As Gloria began to enjoy Tozer and many other beautiful books, our worlds became one.

I hope the books you discover through this book will enrich your life so tremendously that all who meet you will sense that you are a better person because of the books you've read. As you read remember:

Don't read to be big,
  Read to be down to earth.
Don't read to be smart,
  Read to be real.
Don't read to memorize,
  Read to realize.
Don't read to learn,
  Read to sometimes unlearn.
Don't read a lot,
  Read just enough to keep yourself curious and hungry, to learn more, to keep getting younger as you grow older.
  —Charles E. Jones

Great Thoughts
On
Books

Man's Best Friend

Some people think that a dog or a horse is man's best friend, but they are mistaken. I am. And who am I? I am a book. It is true that there are some dogs who love their masters, and who would die for them; but sometimes even loyal dogs have been known to "bite the hand that feeds them." Horses are wonderful creatures, too. Many have been known to "die in their tracks" for their owners: And that's the trouble with horses – they die. You die too, but I don't. I can live until the "end of time". I am the essence of immortality: I am both the child of today and the parent of tomorrow. I am constantly renewing my existence. While faithful dogs and loyal horses have been known to resent abuse, I don't. While there is a limit to patience in dogs and horses, I am immune to such things. You may hurt me but that doesn't change my attitude towards you. I remain steadfast and unserving under all circumstances, and Oh! how some people abuse me.

My covers are broken, sometimes even pulled off, and while I remain naked for years, my heart is untouched. I am as constant as the day you bought me. Loyal and faithful through all the trials and tribulations, yes, and even the neglect, that you put me through. I am the only friend a person has who, though neglected, remains as devoted and as true as though nurtured with love and affection. While you may forget me for years, I always remember you. I am at your beck and call at any hour of the day or night. The knowledge, the inspiration, the comfort to be found with me does not diminish, but increases with time. I can make you laugh as well as cry. I can carry you to the heights of excitement and I can lull you to sleep. And I can accompany you whenever and wherever you go. And if you leave me behind, I will always welcome you back no matter how long you have been away. And if through some act of maliciousness, I am destroyed, you will be able to find me carefully cared for by another. I am your best friend.

I Am A Book

Wordsworth

Dreams, books, are each a world; and books, we know,
Are a substantial world, both pure and good;
Round these, with tendrils strong as flesh and blood,
Our pastime and our happiness will grow.

Often have I sighed to measure
By myself a lonely pleasure,
Sighed to think I read a book
Only read, perhaps, by me.

So passed the time; yet to the nearest town
He daily went with what small overplus
His earnings might supply, and brought away
The book that most had tempted his desires
While at the stall he read. Among the hills
He gazed upon that mighty orb of song,
The divine Milton.

So the foundations of his mind were laid
In such communion, not from terror free.
While yet a child, and long before his time,
Had he perceived the presence and the power
Of greatness; and deep feelings had impressed
Great objects in his mind, with portraiture
And color so distinct, that in his mind
They lay like substances, and almost seemed
To haunt the bodily sense. He had received
A precious gift; for as he grew in years
With these impressions, he would still compare
All his remembrances, thoughts, shapes, and forms;
And being still unsatisfied with aught
Of dimmer character, he thence attained
An active power to fasten images
Upon his brain; and on their pictured lines
Intensely brooded, even till they acquired
The liveliness of dreams.

Emerson

Books are the best type of influence of the past, and perhaps we shall get at the truth – learn the amount of this influence more conveniently – by considering their value alone . . . the scholar of the first age received into him the world around; brooded thereon; gave it the new arrangement of his own mind and uttered it again. It came into him life; it went out from him truth. It came to him short-lived actions; it went out from him immortal thoughts. It came to him business; it went from him poetry. It was dead facts; now it is quick thought. It can stand, and it can go. It now endures, it now flies, it now inspires. Precisely in proportion to the depth of mind from which it issued so high does it soar, so long does it sing.

Walt Whitman

Then falter not, O book, fulfil your destiny.
You not a reminiscence of the land alone.
You too as a lone bark cleaving the ether, purpos'd
I know not whither, yet ever full of faith.

In Cabin'd Ships at Sea

Camerado, this is no book,
Who touches this touches a man, . . .
It is I you hold and who holds you,
I spring from the pages into your arms.

So Long

Shakespeare

O, let my books be then the eloquence
And dumb presagers of my speaking breast;
Who plead for love and for recompense
More than that tongue that more hath more express'd.

Books: Buy the Best

Charles Haddon Spurgeon

If a man can purchase but very few books, my first advice to him would be, let him purchase the very best. If he cannot spend much, let him spend well. The best will always be the cheapest. Leave mere dilutions and attenuations to those who can afford such luxuries. Do not buy milk and water, but get condensed milk, and put what water you like to it yourself. This age is full of word-spinners – professional book-makers, who hammer a grain of matter so thick that it will cover a five-acre sheet of paper; these men have their uses, as good-beaters have, but they are of no use to you. Farmers on our coast used to cart wagon-loads of sea-weed and put them upon their land; the heaviest part was the water: now they dry the weeds, and save a world of labour and expense. Don't buy thin soup; purchase the essence of meat. Get much in little. Prefer books which abound in what James Hamilton used to call "Bibline," or the essence of books. You require accurate, condensed, reliable, standard books, and should make sure that you get them.

Books: Choose the Best

C. C. Colton

With books, as with companions, it is of more consequence to know which to avoid than which to choose: for good books are as scarce as good companions, and, in both instances, all that we can learn from bad ones is, that so much time has been worse than thrown away. That writer does the most who gives his reader the *most* knowledge and takes from him the *least* time. That short period of a short existence which is rationally employed is that which alone deserves the name of life; and that portion of our life is most rationally employed which is occupied in enlarging our stock of truth and of wisdom.

Books: The Great Legacy

Addison

Books are the legacies that a great genius leaves to mankind, which are delivered down from generation to generation, as presents to the posterity of those who are yet unborn. All other arts of perpetuating our ideas continue but a short time. Statues can last but a few thousands of years, edifices fewer, and colours still fewer than edifices Michaelangelo, Fontana, and Raphael will hereafter be what Phidias, Vitruvius, and Apelles are at present, – the names of great statuaries, architects, and painters whose works are lost. The several arts are expressed in mouldering materials. Nature sinks under them, and is not able to support the ideas which are impressed upon it.

The circumstance which gives authors an advantage above all these great masters is this, that they can multiply their originals; or rather can make copies of their works, to what number they please, which shall be as valuable as the originals themselves.

Of all the diversions of life, there is none so proper to fill up its empty spaces as the reading of useful and entertaining authors.

Reading is to the mind what exercise is to the body. As by the one, health is preserved, strengthened, and invigorated; by the other, virtue (which is the health of the mind) is kept alive, cherished, and confirmed.

Greats On Books

A library is true fairyland, a very palace of delight, a haven of repose from the storms and troubles of the world. Rich and poor can enjoy it alike, for here, at least, wealth gives no advantage.

—Avebury

The colleges, whilst they provide us with libraries, furnish no professor of books; and I think no chair is so much wanted.

—Emerson

I conceive that books are like men's souls, divided into sheep and goats. Some few are going up, and carrying us up, heavenward; calculated, I mean, to be of priceless advantage in teaching, in forwarding the teaching of all generations. Others, a frightful multitude, are going down, down; doing ever the more and the wider and the wilder mischief.

—Thomas Carlyle

Reading books in one's youth is like looking at the moon through a crevice; reading books in middle age is like looking at the moon in one's courtyard; and reading books in old age is like looking at the moon on an open terrace. This is because the depth of benefits of reading varies in proportion to the depth of one's own experience.

—Chang Ch'ao

Greats On Books

Some read to think—these are rare; some to write—these are common; and some read to talk—and these form the great majority. The first page of an author not unfrequently suffices all the purposes of this latter class, of whom it has been said that they treat books as some do lords: they inform themselves of their *titles*, and then boast of an intimate acquaintance.

—Colton

Employ your time in improving yourselves by other men's documents; so shall you come easily by what others have laboured hard for. Prefer knowledge to wealth; for the one is transitory, the other perpetual.

—Socrates

Sentences are like sharp nails which force truth upon our memory.

—Diderot

Of all the inanimate objects, of all men's creations, books are the nearest to us, for they contain our very thoughts, our ambitions, our indignations, our illusions, our fidelity to truth, and our persistent leaning toward error. But most of all they resemble us in their precarious hold on life.

—Joseph Conrad

The Love of Books

Book love, my friends, is your pass to the greatest, the purest, and the most perfect pleasure that God has prepared for His creatures. It lasts when all other pleasures fade. It will support you when all other recreations are gone. It will last until your death. It will make your hours pleasant to you as long as you live.

—Anthony Trollope

What a joy there is in a good book, writ by some great master of thought, who breaks into beauty as in summer the meadow into grass and dandelions and violets with geraniums and manifold sweetness.

—Theodore Parker

Books—you are wonderful. In you live the hope, the comfort, the philosophy, the glory, the peace, the reward of a world. You line the edge of my life. As I view you—of a thouand lives expressed and of a hundred thousand thoughts revealed—I say that come what may, so long as I stick to you, I shall not be entirely alone.

—George Matthew Adams

The peace of great books be for you,
Stains of pressed clover leaves on pages,
Bleach of the light of years held in leather.

—Carl Sandburg, *For You*

A Book
I'd Like
To Share

The Light and the Glory

by Peter Marshall and David Manuel
Recommended by: Dick Anthony,
President, Indiana Mills & Mfg., Inc.

I have long been convinced of the strong Christian heritage of the United States and of the faith of our forefathers. However, through extensive research, Peter Marshall and David Manuel have brought a new dimension to one of the most exciting periods of history by bringing to light some rare – even obscure – literary collections. For example, some excerpts from the pen of Christopher Columbus, never before published in English, show the hand of God upon his heart:

"It was the Lord who put into my mind (I could feel his hand upon me) the fact that it would be possible to sail from here to the Indies. All who heard of my project rejected it with laughter, ridiculing me. There is no question that the inspiration was from the Holy Spirit, because He comforted me with rays of marvelous inspiration from the Holy Scriptures."

Other exciting excerpts from the personal diary of George Washington, commonly thought to be a Deist, prove his strong faith in Christ as Savior: "Thou gavest Thy Son to die for me and has given me assurance of salvation upon my repentance and sincerely endeavoring to conform my life to His Holy precepts and example."

Every Christian will thank the authors for a fine job in presenting the spiritual aspects of the founding of a great nation. *The Light and the Glory* is a challenge to all Americans to protect the rich heritage that God has given.

Iacocca, An Autobiography,

by Lee Iacocca with William Novak
Recommended by: Orville E. Beal,
Former Chairman, Prudential Life Insurance Co.,
Recipient of the National Assn. of Life
Underwriters' John Newton Russell Award

One of the finest books I have read in the past ten years (which would include about forty books per year) is Iacocca's autobiography. It is a book which is inspiring and uplifting. I gained a renewal of faith in America and the basic principles which have made ours a great nation. I was thrilled by his entire story of the heights that can be achieved and the goals that can be attained by the practice of good salesmanship and sound management. Each page is a gem of human experience and philosophy. I was sorry to reach the last page.

"I learned about the strength you can get from a close family life. I learned to keep going, even in bad times. I learned not to despair, even when my world was falling apart. I learned that there are no free lunches. And I learned about the value of hard work. In the end, you've got to be productive. That's what made this country great—and that's what's going to make us great again."

Many times the reading of a book has made the future of a man.

—Ralph Waldo Emerson

The Last Puritan

by George Santayana
Recommended by: James Beggs,
Administrator, NASA

Among my favorite books is *The Last Puritan*, by George Santayana. *The Last Puritan*, and similarly *Persons and Places*, which he wrote later, is reflective of the genius of George Santayana in both Philosophy and Literature:

"Yet there were moments when the intensity of Oliver's inner life broke through to the surface. His ideas then ceased to be straggling and clumsy and merely refractory, and came out in strong words. After all, his education had been excellent; he was at home on the higher levels of feeling and knowledge, and had hardly been contaminated at all by the cheap sentiment and catch-words of the day. Beyond that, he possessed by nature an incorruptible spirit, hating compromises and vagueness, and not afraid to be cruel in the interest of truth.

"It was during these days, in a moment of intellectual euphoria, that he composed the 'thesis' on Plato which was the occasion of my great interest in him, and indirectly the first cause of this book. He had been reading the *Phaedrus* and the *Symposium*, and had dutifully made a correct, if rather meagre, summary of their doctrine; but personal comments were asked for; and it was here that, for once, he let himself go. It was not the spirit of Plato, nor of Emerson, his predecessor in that student's chamber, that now descended on Oliver; it was his own spirit that inspired him."

Reflections on the Revolution in France

by Edmund Burke
Recommended by: E. Calvin Beisner,
Editor, Discipleship Journal, Navigators

This book has perhaps had a greater effect on my thought in recent years than any other one book. In it Burke argued that the sentiments underlying the French Revolution were a grave danger to the peaceful relations and genuine rights of men. He predicted with stunning accuracy the artrocities that would be done in the name of the "rights of men" that were dreamed up by the revolutionaries in a fit of madness that forgot the real rights of life, liberty, and property.

It was largely through the mind of Burke that the great principles of political philosophy that underlie modern conservatism were passed on. He understood especially that as T. S. Eliot put it in his *Christianity and Culture* in à world of fallen men compromise is a necessary virtue, not a hateful evil. With the possible exception of *The Federalist Papers* there simply is no better primer on political ethics than Burke's *Reflections*.

Burke protested against dreamers who were so taken up with their theories about the rights of man that they have totally forgot his nature.

Burke cavilled against the revolutionaries of his day by whom "the whole chain and continuity of the commonwealth would be broken" and after whose work "No one generation could link with the other. Men would become little better than the flies of a summer."

He made it his "settled maxim never entirely nor at once to depart from antiquity." Thus Burke wrote, "A disposition to preserve and an ability to improve, taken together, would be my standard of a statesman."

The Story of Philosophy

by Will Durant
Recommended by: Terrell Bell,
Former Secretary, Department of Education

"The first counsel, then, is Life before books; and the second is, Text before commentary. Read the creators rather than the expositors and the critics. 'Only from the authors themselves can we receive philosophic thoughts: therefore whoever feels himself drawn to philosophy must seek out its immortal teachers in the still sanctuary of their own works.' One work of genius is worth a thousand commentaries.

"What one human being can be to another is not a very great deal; in the end everyone stands alone and the important thing is, who it is that stands alone. . . . The happiness which we receive from ourselves is greater than that which we obtain from our surroundings. . . . The world in which a man lives shapes itself chiefly by the way in which he looks at it. . . . Since everything which exists or happens for a man exists only in his consciousness, and happens for him alone, the most essential thing for a man is the constitution of his consciousness. . . . Therefore it is with great truth that Aristotle says, 'To be happy means to be self-sufficient.'"

But the images of men's wits and knowledges remain in books, exempted from the wrong of time, and capable of perpetual renovation.
                                                                        – Francis Bacon

The Book of Knowledge

Published by Grolier
Recommended by: Melvin Belli, Attorney

The name of a book that would help others achieve and learn:

It isn't one book. It is a set of books, because to routinely know but to forget the reason thereof makes building other answers impossible!

The Book of Knowledge is a set of books like an encyclopedia, but it's different from an encyclopedia or such in that it shows more of how to do something rather than what the something is. It isn't fact knowledge as much as modus operandi.

I think one of the most important things a lawyer must have, beside knowing a little law and having a modicum of honesty, is imagination.

Don't tell me how many "box cars stretched out it would take to reach the moon." Show me a diagram instead.

My *Modern Trials*, which is used by so many lawyers now in their demonstrative evidence, is based upon showing rather than telling. It's a procedure rather than a rote fact or almanac.

If I know where to look for something, how to look for something, how to add that something to something else, then I'll come up with my own addition and answers.

Give me the tools to make it, and I'll prepare you a handsome desk. Give me pieces of lumber without directions or imagination, and I'll return the lumber to you in its original state – or maybe even despoiled.

I think *The Book of Knowledge* precipitated me in later years after law school into authoring my books on demonstrative evidence, civil and criminal and *Modern Trials*.

My Melia, now 11, seems to be following – so far – the same course.

A Man Called Peter

by Catherine Marshall
Recommended by: Raymond Berry,
Coach, New England Patriots,
Member, Pro Football Hall of Fame

As a teenager, I picked up a copy of Catherine Marshall's book, *A Man Called Peter*. When Peter Marshall experienced God's "tap on the shoulder," as described in the book, that stuck in my memory.

At the time, I really had no idea what it meant to know God personally through Jesus Christ. This was to be an experience later in my own life. I can't help but wonder if somehow reading about Peter Marshall's "tap on the shoulder" helped me to recognize the same experience years later.

"Choose ye this day whom you will serve." *Joshua 24:15* or in the New Testament:

"No man can serve two masters . . . God and mammon," has a deep significance. *Matthew 6:24.*

"Let me remind you that God does not send anyone to Hell. He permits the soul a choice . . . and if a human being has chosen to gratify the lusts of the flesh rather than the longings of the spirit. . . .

that soul may have to be left with that choice!

What have you chosen?

What are you choosing – day by day?

The proof of how real Jesus knew Hell to be is that He came to earth to save us from it."

Only three things are necessary to make life happy: the blessing of God, books, and a friend.

– Lacordaire

Lives of the Saints

by A. Butler, edited by Thurston Atwater
Recommended by: The Honorable Genevieve Blatt,
Senior Judge, Commonwealth Court of Penna.

The first book from which I can remember my
Mother reading to me was a child's edition of Butler's
famous "Lives of the Saints". That was also the first book
which I recall reading, myself, and I still refer frequently to the large four-volume edition. Great literature it may not be, but a great inspiration it has surely
been!

All of the people whose lives were recounted in this
book were heroic, in the fullest and finest sense of
that honored word. Some were great leaders in the
world, others were humble followers. Some were men
and some were women, and some were even children
who never reached adulthood. There were people of
all races and of all nationalities. Many lived in ancient
times but a few were almost contemporaries. There
were rich and poor, members of every profession and
occupation. Among them were even drifters and beg-
gars and not a few with criminal records. But all of those
people came to love God intensely and, at least most
of the time, tried their best to serve Him well, wherever they were, whatever was their particular state in
life and in spite of the many trials and temptations they
all encountered. In this effort, of course, all of them
obviously succeeded so well that they are now believed
to be surely enjoying the reward He promised for all
who live their lives on earth according to His precepts:
eternal life with Him. Heroes and heroines they were,
every one of them! And I have always enjoyed reading
about them!

The Hidden Persuaders

by Vance Packard
Recommended by: Jack E. Bobo, Executive Sec.,
The National Association of Life Underwriters

Perhaps more than any other influence, Vance Packard's little book, *The Hidden Persuaders*, has helped me to package ideas and concepts more effectively. It has helped me to be more aware of communicating what I really mean, rather than false impressions.

One example in the book that comes to mind is the experience of a beer company surveying their marketplace as to customer preferences for their light or dark beer. The results were puzzling until they realized that the real question they were asking people was "do you buy our cheap beer or our expensive beer?" Not many people will admit to a preference for cheap stuff. The book provides great insight into the art of persuasion.

"The triggers would be needed once the real motivations were diagnosed. They could get guidance on this matter of triggers from Clyde Miller's book *The Process of Persuasion*, where it was pointed out that astute persuaders always use word triggers and picture triggers to evoke desired responses. Once a response pattern is established in terms of persuasion, then you can persuade people in wholesale lots, because all of us, as Professor Miller pointed out are "creatures of conditioned reflex." In his view the crux of all persuasion jobs, whether selling soft drinks or a political philosophy, is to develop these conditional reflexes by flashing on trigger words, symbols, or acts.

A drop of ink may make a million think.

—Byron

The Power of Positive Thinking

by Norman Vincent Peale
Recommended by: Edward R. Book, CEO,
Hershey Entertainment & Resort Company

Let me suggest that it is very difficult to pull out one publication and indicate that it was the foundation for a lifetime.

I believe that we tend to respond to and utilize different publications at different times in our life. Peter Drucker's *Management*, from the late 50's; Peter Drucker's *Managing in Turbulent Times*, from the 70's; *Megatrends* and *In Search of Excellence*, all would be business-oriented publications which I found to be very useful in my business environment. However, were I to suggest one book which has been with me for many years and that I return to in many different situations, I'd suggest that Norman Vincent Peale's *The Power of Positive Thinking* can help see you through many stormy days.

The encouragement to hang on just a little longer, to persist, to wait for the next surprise which life might bring you is the encouragement which we all need – I believe – regardless of the environment in which we are working. Therefore, I would say that Peale's *Positive Thinking* would be the book I have profited from the most over the long term.

"All through its pages, the Bible talks about vitality and force and life. The supreme over-all word of the Bible is life, and life means vitality – to be filled with energy. Jesus stated the key expression, ". . . I am come that they might have life, and that they might have it more abundantly." (John 10:10) This does not rule out pain or suffering or difficulty, but the clear implication is that if a person practices the creative and re-creative principles of Christianity he can live with power and energy."

Chief Executive Officers

Reflexions ou Sentences et Maximes Morales: Reflexions Diverses

by Francois de La Rochefoucauld
Recommended by: Philip E. Lippincott,
CEO, Scott Paper Company

I believe the book that has had the most effect on me is La Rochefoucauld's *Reflexions*. These maxims have helped to keep me in touch with the verities of human nature and life.

Autoconditioning: The New Way to a Successful Life

by Hornell Hart
Recommended by: J. W. McLean,
Chairman, Liberty, the Bank of Mid-America

This book has indeed had an impact upon my life. I not only recommend it to aspiring, young leaders, but also keep a supply on hand to give away, when appropriate.

In Search of Excellence

by Thomas J. Peters & Robert H. Waterman, Jr.
Recommended by: Michael D. Rose,
CEO, Holiday Inns

Chief Executive Officers

Memoirs of the Second World War

by Winston Churchill; and,

Footprints of God

by Arthur I. Brown
Recommended by: Richard Zimmerman,
CEO, Hershey Foods

Ship of the Line

by C. S. Forester
Recommended by: John Woodhouse,
CEO, Sysco

The Power of Positive Thinking

by Norman Vincent Peale
Recommended by: Dick De Camara,
CEO, Midas Muffler

Decline and Fall of the Roman Empire

by Edward Gibbon
Recommended by: Daniel Boorstin,
Librarian of Congress, Historian

Edward Gibbon's *Decline and Fall of the Roman Empire* radiates the author's enchantment with the grandeur of Rome.

It awakened me to what the writing of history could be.

Gibbon was an amateur, and I think that is the greatest vocation of all, for an amateur is a lover, and a lover is a person who does something not because he gets paid for it but because he can't help it and he must do it.

Gibbon was not a dogmatist. His humanity was broad and he saw experience as something that was iridescent, which had a different meaning depending on where you stood or where you sat. In that way, he opened the world in ways a dogmatic historian never could.

In my study at home, where I still do my writing and try to be a historian myself, I have an engraving of Edward Gibbon, who looks down at me with his triple chin and encourages me to do some of the things he did.

"To read with attention, exactly to define the expressions of our author, never to admit a conclusion without comprehending its reason, often to pause, reflect, and interrogate ourselves, these are so many advices which it is easy to give, but difficult to follow. The same may be said of that almost evangelical maxim of forgetting friends, country, religion, of giving merit its due praise, and embracing truth wherever it is to be found."

—Gibbon

Mayors

Boss

by Mike Royko
Recommended by: William Donald Schaefer,
Mayor of Baltimore, Maryland

Boss profiles a man, Mayor Richard Daley of Chicago, who cared about his city. Mayor Daley took pride in his work and his achievements, always remembering that it was the people who made it all a reality. He dedicated his life to making Chicago a better place in which to live.

Boss shows that by means of sheer will-power, perseverance, total dedication and luck, one man can make a difference in the life of a city. Mayor Daley did not achieve the impossible, but he touched the lives of many people, and he left many better off than they were before he became Mayor of Chicago. *Boss* is an inspiring work about an inspiring man.

I Dare You

by William Danforth
Recommended by: Joseph Daddona,
Mayor of Allentown, Pennsylvania

One of the earliest books I recall which influenced my way of thinking was a book called *I Dare You*. I was in my early childhood years at the time and it impressed me tremendously with the philosophy that anybody, regardless of origin or limitations, could be "great" at something if he "dared himself" to do what had to be done to reach that greatness.

The Last Lion

by William Manchester
Recommended by: Frank Borman,
President, Eastern Airlines

I am an avid reader, and one book I would highly recommend to young readers is *The Last Lion*, by William Manchester. It is a biography of Churchill and would serve as an inspiration to any reader.

"The scope of his explorations was broadening – 'I read three or four books at a time to avoid tedium' – and he was poring over Schopenhauer, Malthus, Darwin, Aristotle (on politics only), Henry Fawcett's *Political Economy*, William Lecky's *European Morals and Rise and Influence of Rationalism*, Pascal's *Provincial Letters*, Adam Smith's *Wealth of Nations*, Bartlett's *Familiar Quotations*, Liang's *Modern Science and Modern Thought*, Victor-Henri Rochefort's *Memoirs*, the memoirs of the Duc de Saint Simon, and Henry Hallam's *Constitutional History*. Incredibly, he asked his mother to send him all one hundred volumes of the *Annual Register*, the record of British public events founded by Burke. He explained that he wanted to know 'the detailed Parliamentary history (Debates, Divisions, Parties, cliques & caves) of the last 100 years.' Jennie balked at the expense – fourteen shillings a volume – but she did send twenty-seven. In using them, he first set down his opinion of an issue, then studied the debates. By this practice he hoped 'to build up a scaffolding of logical and consistent views which will perhaps tend to the creation of a logical and consistent mind. Of course the *Annual Register* is valuable only for its facts. A good knowledge of these would arm me with a sharp sword. Macaulay, Gibbon, Plato etc. must train the muscles to wield that sword to the greatest effect.'"

Human Personality

by F. W. H. Myers
Recommended by: Dorthea Brande,
Author, Wake Up & Live

I found the idea which set me free. I was not consciously looking for it. I was engaged on a piece of research in quite another field. But I came across a sentence in the book I was reading. *Human Personality*, by F. W. H. Myers, which was so illuminating that I put the book aside to consider all the ideas suggested in that one penetrating hypothesis. When I picked up the book again I was a different person. Every aspect, attitude, relation of my life was altered.

Myers made a theorizing comment which is of immense value to everyone who hopes to free himself of his bondage to failure. He points out that the ordinary shyness and tentativeness with which we all approach novel action is entirely removed from the hypnotized subject, who consequently acts instead with precision and self-confidence.

Now the removal of shyness, or mauvaise honte (he wrote), *which hypnotic suggestion can effect, is in fact a* purgation of memory—*inhibiting the recollection of previous failures, and setting free whatever group of aptitudes is for the moment required.*

There is the clue. No sentence was ever more packed with rich implication for those who are in earnest about re-orienting their lives towards success.

Act as if it were impossible to fail.

That is the talisman, the formula, the command of right-about-face which turns us from failure towards success.

Moby Dick

by Herman Melville
Recommended by: Charles L. Brown,
Chairman of the Board, AT&T

I support any worthwhile effort to stimulate reading among young people that will provoke them to think and that will spur them to expand their horizons.

Among the classics that did just that for me were Melville's *Moby Dick* and Twain's *Huckleberry Finn.* Those two novels convey more than meets the eye about basic moral issues and the human condition.

Of an entirely different order, a fairly recent book, *In Search Of Excellence,* by Thomas J. Peters and Robert H. Waterman, Jr., recites the characteristics of highly successful companies. It outlines traits that are deceptively simple in their telling but not so easily attained in the day-to-day corporate world.

"Good management practice today is not resident only in Japan. But, more important, the good news comes from treating people decently and asking them to shine, and from producing things that work. Scale efficiencies give way to small units with turned-on people. Precisely planned R&D efforts aimed at big bang products are replaced by armies of dedicated champions. A numbing focus on cost gives way to an enhancing focus on quality. Hierarchy and three-piece suits give way to first names, shirtsleeves, hoopla, and project-based flexibility. Working according to fat rule books is replaced by everyone's contributing."

The man who does not read good books has no advantage over the man who can't read them.

—Mark Twain

Omar Bradley and Books

General U.S. Army

In school we sat in the one large room, more or less grouped by age and grade. My father moved from group to group, assigning lessons, teaching. He was, without a doubt, a brilliant man. I idolized him. He taught us youngsters individual words – sight reading – before we learned the alphabet. I learned to read very quickly. Perhaps it was because my father was the teacher. When your father is the teacher, there's added incentive to do your homework! He was a strict disciplinarian and stricter on me than the others. Even when I climbed in bed with him to get warm at night, he would give me problems to work out in my head.

He succeeded very quickly in inculcating to me a love for books. After I could read fairly well, I devoured books such as Sir Walter Scott's *Ivanhoe*, Kipling's *Jungle Books*, and the like. I was particularly fascinated by history – tales of the French and Indian Wars, the Revolutionary and Civil wars. I would act out many of these battles on the living-room rug, using dominoes to build forts and empty .22 cartridges to represent lines of soldiers. I made "heavy artillery" from hollow elderberry reeds or brass tubing and would bombard the domino forts with navy beans. In my mock wars, the Americans always won.

Employ your time in improving yourself by other men's writings so that you shall come easily by what others have labored hard for.

– Socrates

Syndicated Columnists

Genius

by Theodore Dreiser
Recommended by: James Kilpatrick,
Columnist, Author

As a boy, yearning to become a newspaperman, I profited from the books of Richard Harding Davis, especially the Gallegher stories. When I was 14 or 15, I read Dreiser's *Genius* and found it a real inspiration toward a career in writing.

Tom Sawyer

by Mark Twain
Recommended by: Mike Royko,
Columnist, Author

Planet in Rebellion

by George Vandeman
Recommended by: Paul Harvey,
Paul Harvey News

When you ask which book has meant most – and narrow it to books presently available – the only one that comes to mind is *Planet in Rebellion*, by George Vandeman.

Columnist George Will's
Top Ten

1. *Bible*

2. *Politics,* by Aristotle

3. *Apology,* and *Crito,* by Plato

4. *Macbeth,* by Shakespeare

5. *The Federalist Papers*

6. *Democracy in America,* by DeTocqueville

7. *The Lincoln-Douglas Debates*

8. *The Great Gatsby,* by F. Scott Fitzgerald

9. *Night,* by Elie Wiesel

10. *Idea of a University,* by Cardinal Newman

P.S. My guilty secret is that I am reading my 62nd P.G. Wodehouse novel, which like all the more than 90 of his novels is long on style but short on mind.

Suicide of the West

by James Burnham
Recommended by: Patrick Buchanan,
Political commentator, columnist

Suicide uncovers the primary causes of the "contraction" of the Western world, which has since dissolved throughout the twentieth century into a handful of nations with the emergence of the Third World, the onset of sophisticated military technology, increasingly complex foreign relations and policies, and other issues crucial to the survival of the world. The book maintains that western suicidal tendencies lie not so much in the lack of resources or military power, but through an erosion in intellectual, moral, and spiritual factors abundant in modern western society and the mainstay of liberal psychology.

"What, then, is the primary function of liberalism in our time? It cannot be supposed that a great ideology . . . has no function . . . Modern liberalism could not have achieved its profound and widespread influence, to which very few citizens of the Western nations are altogether immune, unless it fulfilled a pervasive and compelling need. We finish our circle at our point of beginning: Liberalism is the ideology of Western suicide."

Witness

by Whittaker Chambers
Recommended by: William Buckley,
Editor, National Review

I would certainly mention *Witness*, by Whittaker Chambers, a great historical and spiritual melodrama.

"Men may seek God alone. They must worship him in common. The words of Miguel de Unamuno also express my own conviction: 'A miserere sung in a cathedral by a multitude tormented by destiny is equal to a philosophy.' The God it worships is what a nation is, and how he worships Him defines what a man is. I sought a congregation in which I could worship God as the expression of a common need. For I had not changed from secular to religious faith in order to tolerate a formless good will vaguely tinctured with rationalized theology and social uplift. I was not seeking ethics; I was seeking God. My need was to be a practicing Christian in the same sense that I had been a practicing Communist. I was seeking a community of worship in which a daily mysticism (for I hold that God cannot be known in any other way) would be disciplined and fortified by an orderly, and even practical, spirit and habit of life and the mind. Some instinctive sense of my need, abetted by a memory of a conversation with my grandmother Chambers, which I have written about earlier, drew me powerfully to the Religious Society of Friends, the Quakers."

News Commentators

Catcher in the Rye
by J. D. Salinger
Recommended by: Ted Koppel,
Nightline, ABC

The Guns of August
by Barbara Tuchman
Recommended by: Diane Sawyer,
CBS News

Think and Grow Rich
by Napoleon Hill
Recommended by: Bill Kurtis,
CBS News

Healing and Belief
by Norman Cousins
Recommended by: David Hartman,
ABC, Good Morning America

The Theory of the Leisure Class
by Thortein Veblen
Recommended by: Edwin Newman,

Megatrends

by John Naisbitt
Recommended by: Phillip Caldwell,
CEO, Ford Motor Company

I have found John Naisbitt's *Megatrends* quite useful.

"With the coming of the information society, we have for the first time an economy based on a key resource that is not only renewable but self-generating. Running out of it is not a problem, but drowning in it is. . . . We are drowning in information but starved for knowledge."

"Teleconferencing. That is another trend that will not happen. Talking with people via television cannot begin to substitute for the high touch of a meeting, no matter how rational it is in saving fuel and overhead. If it is of little importance, use teleconference. Be appropriate. But we have to face it: There is no end to meetings."

"In our minds, at least, technology is always on the verge of liberating us from personal discipline and responsibility. Only it never does and it never will."

"Economists predict gloom because they focus on industrial companies; that's like predicting a family's future by watching only the grandparents."

". . . if you can develop the skills of facilitating people's involvement in decision-making processes, you can become a very effective leader in your community and your work. The new leader is a facilitator, not an order giver."

Chief Executive Officers

The Federalist Papers

*by Alexander Hamilton, James Madison
and John Jay
Recommended by: Robert W. Galvin,
CEO, Motorola Center*

My book is *The Federalist Papers*, the compendium
of historic documents by Madison, Hamilton and Jay.

The Precious Present

*by Spencer Johnson, M.D.
Recommended by: D. D. Lennox,
CEO, International Harvester*

The book that I enjoyed the most in the past year is
The Precious Present, by Spencer Johnson, M.D.
The book is a short, easily read story that is intriguing, until you perceive the answer. It has, I believe, a
tremendous message.

Last Temptation of Christ

*by Nikos Kazantzakis
Recommended by: Sol Price,
Chairman of the Board, Price Company*

The Power of Positive Thinking

by Dr. Norman Vincent Peale
Recommended by: Doug Campbell,
President, Hobie Cat

If there is one book that is a little more "equal" than any of the others I have read, I would have to say that *The Power Of Positive Thinking* by Norman Vincent Peale had a great impact on me at an early stage in my career.

I could even go further than that; Peale's book had a strong effect on me in all aspects of my life — not just business. It is really the Golden Rule applied to business.

"'Where love is,' said Tolstoy, 'God is,' and, we might add, where God and love are, there is happiness. So a practical principle in creating happiness is to practice love.

"A genuinely happy man is a friend of mine, H. C. Mattern, who, with his equally happy wife, Mary, travels throughout the country in the course of his work. Mr. Mattern carries a unique business card on the reverse side of which is stated the philosophy which has brought happiness to him and his wife and to hundreds of others who have been so fortunate as to feel the impact of their personalities.

"The card reads as follows: 'The way to happiness: keep your heart free from hate, your mind from worry. Live simply, expect little, give much. Fill your life with love. Scatter sunshine. Forget self, think of others. Do as you would be done by. Try this for a week and you will be surprised.'"

Presidents

Seasons of a Man's Life

by Daniel T. Levinson
Recommended by: Patrick Nettleship,
President, North Pacific Construction Company

Aristotle for Everyone

by Mortimer J. Adler
Recommended by: Lawrence M. Kendall,
President, The Group, Inc., Realtors

The Headmaster's Papers

by Richard A. Hawley
Recommended by: T. C. Parmelee,
President, M&F Advertising

Nothing can supply the place of books. They are cheering or soothing companions in solitude, illness, affliction. The wealth of both continents would not compensate for the good they impart. Let every man, if possible, gather some good books under his roof, and obtain access for himself and family to some social library. Almost any luxury should be sacrificed to this.
– Dr. W. E. Channing: *Self-Culture*

The Success Principle

by Dave Johnson
Recommended by: Paul V. Campbell,
Vice President, MAI

Inspiration and encouragement are essential to strengthen the resolve of anyone facing a monumental business challenge. These factors are analogous to packing food and water to cross the desert.

In books, the thoughts and theories of other men who have faced and overcome significant business challenges – against all the odds – are written down. It's so simple, so inexpensive; and yet, ironically, . . . relatively few managers of men and assets seek inspiration and guidance in the written word.

It happens to me and I'm sure it happens to almost all managers and leaders of men – we let our subconscious feed us negatives. We fail to take remedial action through the power of books to feed us subconscious positive thoughts. Left to it's own inclination, our mind will feed us doubt, fear, negative precedence and cautious thoughts.

I was given a copy of the book, *The Success Principle.* It's odd that someone should simply stretch out their hand and give me a $5.00 book. I wasn't expecting that but it happened. I put the book in my briefcase and went on with my misery.

It was perhaps three weeks before a New York flight offered me the opportunity to quietly read through this delightful little book. I got off that plane positive, renewed, confident.

In Search of Identity:
An Autobiography

by Anwar El Sadat
Recommended by: Richard Capen, Jr.,
Chairman & Publisher, The Miami Herald

Two books appeal to me.

One is an "Autobiography of Values," written by Anwar Sadat several years before his assassination. I found his testimony of faith to be an inspiration. It obviously helped him pass through threats, imprisonment and the incredible pressures of his position in life.

"By then we were allowed to read books, magazines, and newspapers. I read voraciously, finding in every word a novelty – something that opened up new horizons before my very eyes.

"I read more in English than in Arabic. When an idea, a poem, or anything in print appealed to me, I immediately copied it into a notebook that I still keep and really cherish. I call it the Prison Notebook. It includes quotations from world authors – Eastern and Western alike – who have had a marked influence on my life.

"My wide-ranging reading not only broadened my mind and enriched my emotions, it also helped me to know myself better. Through reading I succeeded in overcoming certain nervous troubles which had been caused by my arrest in the small hours in the bitterly cold winters of 1942 and 1946. I had not realized the nature of these nervous 'crises' but I knew that they disturbed by deep spiritual recesses; only when I had engaged in that long soul-searching in prison did my troubles float to the surface of my consciousness."

The other is book is *Psycho-Cybernetics*, which offers practical suggestions for instilling an attitude of positivism.

The Fate of the Earth

by Jonathan Schell
Recommended by: Aloysius G. Casey,
Major General, U.S. Air Force

This is perhaps a curious selection for one who has dedicated most of his adult life to the operation and acquisition of strategic nuclear weapons, but, nonetheless, I found it of great value. Mr. Schell devotes the early part of the book to a detailed discussion of the effect of a massive nuclear weapon exchange upon the planet earth. He makes a sound case that the fate of the human race may well be at stake in such an exchange; concluding, therefore, that we have a moral imperative to preclude its occurrence.

He then proceeds to establish the futility of trying to reverse history and wipe out the knowledge required to build nuclear weapons. In a logical construct, tightly reasoned, he announces the obsolescence of the concept that war is a reasonable means to finally arbitrate conflict between major nation states. However, his prescription for a solution, i.e., revising the political structure of our planet, is not well defined and is perhaps only naive idealism.

The value of this book lies in its clear statement of concerns shared by many of our citizens, church organizations and allies. While I do not share his zeal for world government, I do believe his clear, concise logic is a great contribution to fostering intelligent debate in the most important public issue we face this century. We can only hope that informed public discussion will one day resolve this threat to planet earth.

Think and Grow Rich

by Napoleon Hill
Recommended by: S. Truett Cathy,
President, Chick-fil-A, Inc.

Think and Grow Rich was discovered by me in 1938 through a teacher in high school. I read it and re-read it and tried to apply its principles to my development.

"One of the main weaknesses of mankind is the average man's familiarity with the word 'impossible.' He knows all the rules which will not work. He knows all the things which cannot be done. This book was written for those who seek the rules which have made others successful, and are willing to stake everything on those rules.

"Somewhere in your make-up there lies sleeping the seed of achievement which, if aroused and put into action, would carry you to heights such as you may never have hoped to attain.

"Just as a master musician may cause the most beautiful strains of music to pour forth from the strings of a violin, so may you arouse the genius which lies asleep in your brain, and cause it to drive you upward to whatever goal you may wish to achieve.

"The 'system' denies no one this right, but it does not, and cannot, promise something for nothing, because the system itself is irrevocably controlled by the law of economics which neither recognizes nor tolerates for one second, getting without giving."

A good book contains more real wealth than a good bank.

—Roy L. Smith

Oswald Chambers & Books

A friend of Chambers wrote the following paragraph about an encounter with him:

"For some time I had been in a puzzling cul de sac mentally; continually passing on to others the truth revealed to me. I realized that I lacked the ability to give form in my mind and expression in words to what I knew in my heart. Mr. Chambers asked me what I read. When I told him nothing but the Bible and books directly associated with it, he diagnosed the difficulty at once and said, 'The trouble is you have allowed part of your brain to stagnate for want of use.' Then and there he gave me a list of over fifty books, philosophical, psychological, theological, covering almost every phase of current thought. The outstanding result was a revolution which can only be described as a mental new birth. I entered a land of far distances, which by God's grace is still extending and expanding."

Chambers' intense interest in art and literature, which continued throughout his ministry, was not to be wasted but used in a magnificent way, flavoring all his sermons with an unusual depth and realism. In a letter written in 1907, he reveals his love for communing with the great minds: "My box has at last arrived. My books! I cannot tell you what they are to me – silent, wealthy, loyal, lovers. I do thank God for my books with every fibre of my being . . . I see them all just at my elbow now – Plato, Wordsworth, Myers, Bradley, Halburton, St. Augustine, Browning, Tennyson, Amiel, and the others."

– D. W. Lambert

Whittaker Chambers and
Les Misérables

(From The Witness, 1952)

"I did not understand half the words. How should I know what 'human fatality' meant, or 'social asphyxia'? But when I read those lines, there moved through my mind a stolen music that is the overtone of justice and compassion. A spirit moved upon the page and through my ignorance I sensed that spirit.

"The book, of course, was Victor Hugo's *Les Misérables* —*The Wretched of the Earth*. In its pages can be found the play of forces that carried me into the Communist Party, and in the same pages can be found the play of forces that carried me out of the Communist Party. The roots of both influences are in the same book, which I read devotedly for almost a decade before I even opened a Bible, and which was, in many respects the Bible of my boyhood. I think I can hear a derisive question: 'How can anyone take seriously a man who says flatly that his life has been influenced by Victor Hugo's *Les Misérables*?' I understand; I can only answer that, behind its colossal failings, its melodrama, its windy philosophizing, its clots of useless knowledge, its overblown rhetoric and repellent posturings, which offend me, like everybody else, on almost every page, *Les Misérables* is a great act of the human spirit. And it is a fact that books which fall short of greatness sometimes have a power to move us greatly, especially in childhood when we are least critical and most forgiving, for their very failures confess their humanity. As a boy, I did not know that *Les Misérables* is a *Summa* of the revolt of the mind and soul of modern man against the materialism that was closing over them with the close of the Middle Ages and the rise of industrial civilization – or, as Karl Marx would later teach me to call it: capitalism."

Winston Churchill and Books

exerpts from his correspondence

"I have not yet had any boxing lessons. Perhaps you would not mind me hinting that *my Birthday* is drawing near. I am looking forward to a visit from you on that day. I should rather like 'Gen. Grant's History of the American War.'"   (11/16/1887 – age 13)

"PS   I approach the end of a delightful companionship of six months with Gibbon. Do you think Macaulay will be a worthy successor?"   (12/16/1896 – age 22)

"Rudyard Kipling's new book is I think very inferior and not up to the standard of his other works. Few writers stand the test of success. Rider Haggard – Weyman – Boldrewood are all losing or have already lost their prowess."   (1/7/97)

"I have to thank you for 12 volumes of Macaulay which I shall shortly begin to read. The eighth volume of Gibbon is still unread as I have been lured from its completion by *The Martyrdom of Man* & a fine translation of the Republic of Plato: both of which are fascinating."   (1/14/97)

"I envy Jack – the liberal education of an University. I find my literary tastes growing day by day – and if I only knew Latin & Greek – I think I would leave the army and try and take my degree in History, Philosophy & Economics."   (1/14/97)

"I am half way through Macaulay & you must find me something else as he is not half so solid as Gibbon & I have a good deal of time to read him in. I want Adam Smith's *Wealth of Nations*. I hear a good book *On the Face of the Water* which Barnes is reading." (2/18/97)

The Seven Pillars of Wisdom

by T. E. Lawrence
Recommended by: William E. Colby,
Former Director, Central Intelligence Agency

There are so many books whose eloquence and message have affected all of us that it is very difficult to single one out. I confess I find my own interests chiefly in biographies of individuals who have accomplished a great deal in this world, and there are, of course, many whose careers are an inspiration to us all. I offer you the book by T. E. Lawrence of Arabia, *The Seven Pillars of Wisdom*. The reason I select it is because it reflects a man of courage who is yet sensitive to the totally different cultures in the world, and is determined to use his efforts against those who are oppressing another people. This kind of life can inspire all of us and point out the necessity of courage in all our lives since, as Winston Churchill said, "Courage is the first of the virtues, because upon it depend all the others."

"I am convinced that much of what Lawrence accomplished, perhaps the central importance of his life, derived from the force of his moral example, what was known in an earlier time as 'character.' Mrs. Hardy expressed this best perhaps in a letter to Robert Graves in 1927 about Lawrence: 'I consider him the most marvelous human being I have ever met. It is not his exploits in Arabia that attract me, nor the fact that he is a celebrity: it is his character that is so splendid.'"

—John E. Mack

Tough Times Never Last, But Tough People Do

by Robert H. Schuller
Recommended by: Kenneth Cooper, M.D.,
President, The Cooper Clinic

A book which recently has had an effect on my life was authored by Dr. Schuller and entitled *Tough Times Never Last, But Tough People Do.* In the development of both the Aerobics program and The Aerobics Center in Dallas, there have been multiple times when the problems seemed overwhelming and insurmountable. Yet, as mentioned in Dr. Schuller's book, these tough times don't last. In other words, our problems should make us "better, not bitter."

"Possibility thinking is in actuality the exercise of dynamic creative sanctified *imagination.*

"Sir Edmund Hillary, who attempted to scale Mount Everest, lost one of the members of his team in the failed effort. He returned to a hero's welcome in London, England, where a banquet held in his honor was attended by the lords and ladies and powerful people of the British Empire. Behind the speaker's platform were huge blown-up photographs of Mount Everest. When Hillary arose to receive the acclaim of the distinguished audience, he turned around and faced the mountain and said, 'Mount Everest, you have defeated me. But I will return. And I will defeat you. *Because you can't get any bigger and I can.*'"

The Autobiography of Lincoln Steffens

Recommended by: Norman Cousins,
Former Editor, The Saturday Review,
Faculty Member, University of California

I have a very clear recollection of when I was twelve years old of *The Autobiography of Lincoln Steffens,* the life story of an American reporter, student of ethics and politics, a muckraker in his early twentieth century attempts to reform government.

At that time, parents were giving that book to their children mostly because of the first part where the description of Steffens' childhood was very vivid. Even now I have an unforgettable picture of Steffens' first experience with his pony.

But to me the most exciting part of the book was the description of his career as a muckraker, what happened when he got into journalism, how he got into the engineering of consent in terms of public issues, persuading people, especially in small towns.

I can still see that town meeting in Greenwich, Connecticut, where he went to the blackboard and explained to the townspeople how their town, any small town, really works, and what had to be done if the town, in fact, was to be representative of the people's interest.

That was when I decided to go into journalism.

The way a book is read—which is to say, the qualities a reader brings to a book—can have as much to do with its worth as anything the author puts into it . . . Anyone who can read can learn how to read deeply and thus live more fully.

—Norman Cousins

The Tyranny Of The Urgent

by Charles E. Hummel
Recommended by: Mary C. Crowley,
CEO, Home Interiors and Gifts, Inc.

A book that has had a tremendous influence on my thinking is very small. *The Tyranny Of The Urgent* is the best book on time management that I have ever seen. Here are some of the thoughts from the book:

"When we stop to evaluate, we realize that our dilemma goes deeper than shortage of time. It is basically the problem of priorities. Hard work does not hurt us. We all know what it is to go full speed for long hours totally involved in an important task. The resulting weariness is matched by a sense of achievement and joy. Not hard work, but doubt and misgivings produce anxiety. As we review a month or a year, we become oppressed by the pile of unfinished tasks. We sense easily that we may have failed to do the important. The whims of other people's demands have driven us under the reef of frustration. We confess quite apart from our sins, we have left undone those things which we ought to have done, and done those things which we ought not to have done.

'Your greatest danger is in letting the urgent things crowd out the important.' The problem is that the important task rarely must be done today; or even this week. Extra hours of prayer and Bible study, a visit, careful study of an important book. Those projects can wait, but the urgent task calls for instant action, endless demands and pressure, every hour of the day."

College Football Coaches

Exodus

by Leon Uris
Recommended by: Bill Curry,
Football Coach, Georgia Tech

My choice of a book which has been meaningful to me would be *Exodus*, by Leon Uris. This book taught me to better understand the following:

1. The reality of man's inhumanity to man.

2. How complicated seemingly simple events really are.

3. How powerful the truly committed human spirit can be.

The Royal Road to Romance

by Richard Halliburton
Recommended by: Joe Paterno,
Football Coach, Pennsylvania State Univ.

If my life had been more full of calamity than it has been, I would live it over again to have read the books I did in my youth.

—William Hazlitt

College Football Coaches

Tough Times Never Last, But Tough People Do

by Dr. Robert Schuller
Recommended by: Fred Akers,
Football Coach, University of Texas

Leaves of Gold

Edited by Clyde Francis Lytle
Recommended by: Darrell Royal,
Former Football Coach, University of Texas

I enjoyed reading thoughts from *Leaves of Gold*, edited by Clyde Francis Lytle, because it fit into my haphazard time schedule. During the year that I was coaching, I found short periods of time that I could pick up *Leaves of Gold*, and I benefited from it.

When players tired or wanted to quit, I read from the chapter on Work. I especially used Marie Dressler's comments on cooperation.

Cultivation is necessary to the mind as food is to the body.

– Cicero

The Will to Manage

by Marvin Bower
Recommended by: John B. Curcio,
President, Mack Trucks, Inc.

Although I have read many books and greatly admire the writings of Peter Drucker in particular, the one book I would recommend to aspiring young leaders is *The Will to Manage*, by Marvin Bower, published by McGraw Hill in 1966. The overall moral of this book is that "the key to corporate success is a leader with a strong will to manage, who inspires and requires able people to work purposefully and effectively through simple and traditional managing processes that are integrated into a management program or system tailored to the nature and environment of the business." It further teaches that you must maintain high ethical standards in internal and external relationships, make decisions based on objectively considered facts, continually adjust to the forces at work in your environment, judge people only on the basis of their performance and, thus, finally create an organization with a sense of competitive urgency.

Books are delightful when prosperity happily smiles; when adversity threatens, they are inseparable comforters. They give strength to human compacts, nor are grave opinions brought forward without books. Arts and sciences, the benefits of which no mind can calculate, depend upon books.

— Richard De Bury

The Art of Thinking

by Abbé Dimnet
from I Dare You!
by William H. Danforth,
Founder of Ralston Purina Company

"Have you read Abbé Dimnet's *The Art of Thinking*? If not, buy it right away. Don't get it from the library. Own it. Lose no time. Its pages fascinatingly lead you into a new mental realm. If you already have a copy, dust it off and read it over again. Stagnant minds are the greatest obstacles to progress.

"Most of the unexplored regions of the world may have been discovered, but what a field lies ahead for the mental Columbus, the thinking Peary, the planning Byrd. Physical adventure promises not half the thrill of mental adventure. Physical life brings happiness, but mental life brings interest – a consuming, absorbing interest. How I pity that person, young or old, who cannot shut out the world, open a book, and go forth on an adventure of romance, travel, biography, history or business. What a shame to see so many mental lives slow down after school days are over, just because people forget the necessity of everlastingly studying if they expect to get anywhere. Theodore Roosevelt died with a book under his pillow, consuming the ideas of others until the very last."

Every man who knows how to read has it in his power to magnify himself, to multiply the ways in which he exists, to make his life full, significant and interesting.

–Aldous Huxley

The One Minute Manager

by Kenneth Blanchard & Spencer Johnson
Recommended by: R. L. Danner,
Chairman, CEO, Shoney's, Inc.

A book title that I would recommend that I have profited by during my career is *The One Minute Manager.*

TAKE A MINUTE

LOOK AT YOUR GOALS

LOOK AT YOUR PERFORMANCE

SEE IF YOUR BEHAVIOR MATCHES YOUR GOALS

An ordinary man can in the ordinary course, without any undue haste or putting any pressure upon his taste, surround himself with two thousand books, all in his own language, and thenceforward have at least one place in the world in which it is possible to be happy.

—Augustine Birrell

Tough Times Never Last
But Tough People Do!

by Robert H. Schuller
Recommended by: Fisher DeBerry,
Football Coach, U.S. Air Force Academy

The book that has had the most powerful impact on me recently is Bob Schuller's *Tough Times Never Last, But Tough People Do!* I am a great follower and advocate of Dr. Schuller's positive thinking philosophy and have read a lot of his material. I don't know of any line of work that has any more ups and downs than the coaching profession. A lot of times there are highs and lows within the same day, but this book has been a great source of strength to me during my first year as head coach at the Academy.

"The storm has passed. The birds are singing. The night is over. Tough times never last. Tough people do! That's really true if we live moment by moment, day by day, in complete surrender to God in prayer. Through prayer, God gives the power to hold on in tough times until the breakthrough comes.

But those who wait on the LORD
Shall renew their strength;
They shall mount up with wings like eagles,
They shall run and not be weary,
They shall walk and not faint
(Is. 40:31)."

How to Win Friends & Influence People

by Dale Carnegie
Recommended by: Rich DeVos, CPAE,
President, Amway Corporation

I can think of one book – and course – which has influenced me over the years. I took the course and read the book, *How to Win Friends & Influence People*. Even today, I recommend that Amway employees and independent distributors learn the basics of inter-personal communication through such a book or course.

"If a man's heart is rankling with discord and ill feeling toward you, you can't win him to your way of thinking with all the logic in Christendom. Scolding parents and domineering bosses and husbands and nagging wives ought to realize that people don't want to change their minds. They can't be forced or driven to agree with you or me. But they may possibly be led to, if we are gentle and friendly, ever so gentle and ever so friendly."

"There is one all-important law of human conduct. If we obey that law, we shall almost never get into trouble. In fact, that law, if obeyed, will bring us countless friends and constant happiness. But the very instant we break the law, we shall get into endless trouble. The law is this: *Always make the other person feel important.* John Dewey, as we have already noted, said that the desire to be important is the deepest urge in human nature; and William James said: 'The deepest principle in human nature is the craving to be appreciated.' As I have already pointed out, it is this urge that differentiates us from the animals. It is this urge that has been responsible for civilization itself."

Chief Executive Officers

In Search of Excellence

by Thomas Peters & Robert Waterman, Jr.
Recommended by: James O'Connor,
CEO, Commonwealth Edison

Getting to Yes

by Roger Fisher & William Ury
Recommended by: Debrah Charatan-Berger,
President, Bach Realty Inc.

Profiles in Courage

by John F. Kennedy
Recommended by: Ian Rolland,
CEO, Lincoln Life

Atlas Shrugged

by Ayn Rand
Recommended by: Paul Oreffice,
CEO, Dow Chemical

Common Sense –
The Call to Independence

by Thomas Paine
Recommended by: Dr. Greg Dixon,
Pastor, Indianapolis, Indiana

This book, written by one of the founders of American Independence, is a primer on the philosophical necessity of independence from Great Britain and the formation of a republican form of government. In spite of the fact that England afforded the freest government on earth at that time, Paine told Americans that this was not enough. He challenged his generation to enjoy more liberty than any other people on earth up to that time had experienced. He obliterated the English Constitution by revealing that it continued and extended the monarchy in a despotic grip over the lives of its citizens. Paine gives one of the greatest evidences that America was founded as one nation under God by answering the question, "But where, say some, is the King of America?" "I'll tell you, friend, He reigns above . . ." Of equal importance with his attack on kingship is his insistence that "Republicanism is the only system of government capable of preserving freedom." He also convinced Americans that they could win victory over England, and that they must not fear to be free.

Paine gives the manifest destiny of America in these words: "The reformation was preceded by the discovery of America, as if the Almighty graciously meant to open a sanctuary to the persecuted in future years." This book caused me to have a greater love of liberty than ever before.

Great Americans
Patrick Henry and Books

Henry's books as listed in the inventory after his death comprise over 225 well chosen volumes relating to religion, history, law, politics, classical literature, and other topics. But there are none by such deistic writers as Voltaire and Rousseau. Among the typical titles, often incorrectly spelled in the court records, are Homer's *Ilias, Don Quck Zotte, The Compleat English Farmer and Modern Farmer's Guild, Essays on Slagery*, Bonepartte's *Camphain*, Tillotson's *Sermons*, and two volumes of the *Independent Wigg* (Whig). Henry was too occupied with political business when in Williamsburg and Richmond to absorb much of the local deistic thought, and in the secluded back country his religious influences were of the conservative – indeed, rather fundamentalist – type. While he had gone through a period of some religious questioning, by the Red Hill years his views had become decidedly orthodox.   – Robert Douthat Meade

Make It Your Own – Daniel Webster

The opinion of my scholarship was a mistaken one. It was over estimated. I will explain what I mean. Many other students read more than I did and knew more than I did. But so much as I read, I made my own. When a half hour or an hour, at most, had elapsed, I closed my book and thought over what I had read. If there was anything peculiarly interesting or striking in the passage, I endeavored to recall it and lay it up in my memory, and commonly could effect my object. Then, if in debate or conversation afterwards, any subject came up on which I had read something. I could talk very easily so far as I had read and then I was very careful to stop. Thus, greater credit was given me for extensive and accurate knowledge than I really possessed.

Growing Strong in the Seasons of Life

by Charles Swindoll
Recommended by: Terry Donahue,
Head Football Coach, UCLA

The book that has been a source of inspiration in my life is *Growing Strong in the Seasons of Life*.

When the rigors of coaching and the pressures involved in this profession begin to take their toll, I have found this book to be inspirational, relaxing and of value to me.

"This is a book about the recurring seasons of life. It offers a series of suggestions and ideas to help you read God's signals with a sensitive heart. Quietly and deliberately, we'll walk together through each scene, pondering the subtle shading as well as the obvious broad brush strokes from the Artist's hand. Let's take our time and leave room for our feelings to emerge. Let's sing in harmony with the Composer's music. Let's drink in the beauty of His handiwork. It will take time, so let's not hurry.

"Our journey begins in the winter, a season of quiet reverence. This is followed by spring, a season of refreshing and encouraging renewal. Then comes summer, a season of enjoyable and much-needed rest. Finally, we'll stroll through autumn, a season of nostalgic reflection. Our hope is to grow stronger and taller as our roots dig deeper in the soft soil along the banks of the river of life. And let's not fear the winds of adversity! The gnarled old twisted trees, beaten and buffeted by wind and weather along the ocean shores, tell their own stories of consistent courage. May God make us strong as the winds whip against us, my friend. Roots grow deep when the winds are strong. Let's commit ourselves to growing strong in the seasons of life."

Lee, The Last Years

by Charles Brayson Flood
Recommended by: Vincent Dooley,
Athletic Director & Head Football Coach, Univ. of Georgia

I have had the opportunity to read many books that I felt were inspiring and of great personal benefit to me. Since this is the case, I will offer you the last book I've read that I thought was very inspiring.

Charles Brayson Flood's *Lee, The Last Years*, does a marvelous job of filling in the gap after Appomattox of one of the most famous figures in American history. The book reveals that Robert E. Lee, more than any other American, through his compassion, generosity and conciliation helped to heal the wounds between the North and the South after the war. Though Lee is best known as a military genius, his last years have been described as "his finest hour." This is certainly one of the books that has been special to me.

"One of these incoming younger students was so taken aback by Lee's gentleness that he thought he was in the wrong office and that this was not the recent Confederate commander: 'He was so gentle, kind, and almost motherly, that I thought there must be some mistake about it.' Once this boy was convinced that he was indeed talking with Robert E. Lee, he saw something more. 'It looked as if the sorrow of a whole nation had been collected in his countenance, and as if he were bearing the grief of his whole people. It never left his face, but was ever there to keep company with the kindly smile.'"

Pro Football

The Lou Gehrig Story, and
The George Washington Carver Story

Recommended by: Roger Staubach,
All-Pro Quarterback, Dallas Cowboys

These were two books that I read when I was younger and that had a great influence on me.

Bodyguard of Lies

by Anthony Cave Brown
Recommended by: Dan Reeves,
Coach, Denver Broncos

The Hairy Ape

by Eugene O'Neill
Recommended by: Frank Emanuel,
Linebacker, Miami Dolphins and New Orleans Saints

This book taught me that even if man is at the bottom of the chain, if he is contributing, then he is worthwhile and belongs.

Mere Christianity

by C. S. Lewis
Recommended by: Merrill Douglass,
Certified Speaking Professional

The power of printed words to alter lives is phenomenal. That is not to say that all books are great. Many, unfortunately, are awful. But some are good. Some are very good. And a few are magnificent; treasures to be read and re-read, adding new value each time. Such a book is *Mere Christianity,* written by C. S. Lewis in 1943, and still a strong seller today.

An unusual book, with no ax to grind, *Mere Christianity* is simply a clear explanation of what Christianity is all about. It is totally devoid of religious dogma and denominational bias, written as much for non-believers as for those already committed to Jesus Christ.

C. S. Lewis is indisputably an intellectual, a philosopher, a deep thinker. Yet, he also has the rare ability to discuss profound issues with uncommon clarity. There is no pedantic prose, no erudite ego. With simple language and logic he explains the foundation for belief. The more you read, the more you understand what God wants us to be.

The mark of a great book is that it improves with each reading. You never tire of it. It touches you intellectually and emotionally. It inspires you to become better, to grow and develop. It motivates you to act upon its ideas, to make them a part of your life.

Mere Christianity does all this and more. Only the Bible has had a greater impact on me. This book helped me better understand how I fit in the cosmic order of events and to understand better my role as a Christian. Thank you, C. S. Lewis, for helping unlock the peace, the power and the promise of Christianity.

The Plays of William Shakespeare

Recommended by: Honorable John C. Dowling, Judge, Dauphin County, Pennsylvania

I have been a prolific reader all my life and try to get through at least one book a week. Actually, using the term in its broadest sense, as having made life more meaningful, I have profited from hundreds of books. If I must choose one, I think it would be *The Plays of William Shakespeare*. They have broadened my knowledge of human nature, sustained me in times of trial, increased my appreciation of life and encouraged my efforts to do what is right. As Ben Jonson said, "He was not of an age, but for all time."

Opportunity

from "Julius Caesar"

There is a tide in the affairs of men,
Which, taken at the flood, leads on to fortune;
Omitted, all the voyage of their life
Is bound in shallows, and in miseries.
On such a full sea are we now afloat;
And we must take the current when it serves,
Or lose our ventures.

— Shakespeare

The Discoverers

by Daniel J. Boorstin
Recommended by: Arthur C. Eckerman,
Educator

Where can one find a book which introduces and describes famous people of all times, their thinking and their contributions to civilization – a book about man and his discoveries?

A book has been published recently by a well known historian, teacher and philosopher – Daniel J. Boorstin, presently the Librarian of Congress. Among his many publications will stand out *The Discoverers*, a history of man's search to know his world and himself. It is a veritable smorgasbord of fascinating people from all walks of life – their lives and their works. It is a book in which one can turn to any page and find a surfeit of information and knowledge. Only a brief scan of the contents is possible here. One is about TIME, another deals with the EARTH and the SEAS, the men who discovered and explored them, a third describes NATURE and the scientists who opened the frontiers of nature to discover its secrets, and a fourth part deals with SOCIETY. This may well be the most interesting section of all, considering mankind and our struggles to survive in today's troubled, changing world.

Boorstin's book *The Discoverers* is not easy to ignore or put aside. "The world we now view from the literate West – the vistas of time, the land and the seas, the heavenly bodies and our own bodies, the plants and animals, history and human societies past and present – had to be opened for us by countless Columbuses." This is what the book is about, discoverers and their motivations. It will indeed enrich one's own life.

That Man Is You

by Louis Evely
Recommended by: Col. Vernon R. Edmondson,
USAF Ret.; Chaplain, New Mexico Military Inst.

Louis Evely's *That Man Is You*, comes as fresh as the dew. This opening phrase is how too much of theology is put in print. It is too hackneyed to catch the beating heart of this book which so delightfully slams home the familiar with a twist of goodwill and humor. Evely employs much loved Scripture worn smooth by repeat readings and sets those passages like new gemstones in a golden framework of words.

Evely is a European Roman Priest with a catholic voice. His message is the Word made human and universal by means of a heart and a willingness to be a scribe in the employ of the Holy Spirit. Each time I pick up this book I know that God still speaks through human personality and that we humans, laced with the Divine, can be used by Him to provoke each other to action.

"Active passivity," indeed! I am passive and feeling all lonely and useless just praying, but not so with God! It is never just prayer.

The author is pithy and pious, but never haranguing nor stringent. His words penetrate and sting, yet leave an aftertaste of love and comfort. His wit and will masterfully blend in unusual phraseology to quicken the reader's interest. Evely reminds us that God's Word is alive and we must be, too.

As a Man Thinketh

by James Allen
Recommended by: Coy Eklund,
Former Chairman, Equitable Life Assurance Society,
Recipient of the National Assn. of Life
Underwriters' John Newton Russell Award

The name of a book that has meant something special to me over the years is one by James Allen, titled *As a Man Thinketh*. It is a tiny book, but one that is full of the kind of thinking and philosophy that have had a deep meaning to me. For example, "A man is what he thinks about all day long." It also puts things in verse so they become indelibly fixed in your memory. Listen to these two:

Mind is the master power that molds and makes,
And man is mind, and evermore he takes
The tool of thought, and shaping what he wills,
Brings forth a thousand joys, a thousand ills.
He thinks in secret, and it comes to pass;
Environment is but his looking glass.

The vision that you glorify in your mind,
The ideal that you enthrone in your heart;
This you will build your life by,
This you will become.

This is the kind of stuff that has filled and motivated me all my working life, and is the kind of thinking I would recommend to young people early in their careers. It is basic to any real success.

Beyond Survival

by Leon Danco
Recommended by: Michael J. Etchison,
President, Twoson Tool Company

This book was a real boost to me at a very crucial time in the transition of leadership in the company my father founded.

It was like reading my dad's autobiography. I felt like Mr. Danco was a long lost friend as I read his description of my father. I discovered through this book that much of what I knew and was experiencing others were also finding to be their frustration.

Mr. Danco aptly describes the business owner/ founder with all his strengths and weaknesses. His book also helps the successor who reads it to understand some important principles about successful transition of leadership within a family owned company.

I learned that my dad's natural instincts were "to acquire not to share, to work not teach, and how to solve problems, not ask for help to solve them."

Mr. Danco gives sound, clear instruction and advice on how to organize for and plan the orderly succession of leadership in a family owned company. Many items are discussed, such as a firm's need for a competent manager, a budget for profit planning, the need to get competent advisors and also a competent, working board of directors to review the performance of the new chief executive officer and provide for continuity of the business future.

The Greatest Miracle in the World

by Og Mandino
Recommended by: Gerry Faust,
Football Coach, University of Notre Dame

A book I would highly recommend to all readers is
The Greatest Miracle in the World, by Og Mandino.

"You are my greatest miracle.
"You are the greatest miracle in the world.
"And now the laws of happiness and success are three.
"Count your blessings! Proclaim your rarity! Go
another mile!
"Be patient with your progress. To count your blessings with gratitude, to proclaim your rarity with pride,
to go an extra mile and then another, these acts are not
accomplished in the blinking of an eye. Yet, that which
you acquire with most difficulty you retain the longest;
as those who have earned a fortune are more careful
of it than those by whom it was inherited.
"And fear not as you enter your new life. Every noble
acquisition is attended with its risks. He who fears to
encounter the one must not expect to obtain the other.
Now you know you are a miracle. And there is no fear
in a miracle."

Books are the quietest and most constant of friends;
they are the most accessible and wisest of counsellors,
and the most patient of teachers.

                                                               —Charles W. Eliot

Sayings of the Fathers

Recommended by: Aaron S. Feinerman,
Feinerman Insurance Agency

My selection, *Sayings of the Fathers*, is a rabbinical tractate also known as *Ethics of the Fathers*. It consists of the favorite maxims of some sixty Rabbis extending over a period of nearly 500 years from 800 B.C.E. to 200 C.E.

These sayings are universal in application and have not lost their power with the passing of time. They give guidance in human conduct and duty.

Here is a quote from the famous scholar, HILLEL:

"Separate not thyself from the congregation; trust not in thyself until the day of thy death; judge not thy neighbor until thou art come into his place; and say not anything which cannot be understood at once, in the hope that it will be understood in the end; neither say, When I have leisure I will study; perchance thou wilt have no leisure."

"Whenever love depends upon some material cause, with the passing away of that cause, the love too passes away; but if it be not dependent upon such a cause, it will not pass away forever."

"Seek not greatness for thyself, and court not honor: let thy works exceed thy learning, and crave not after the table of kings; for thy table is greater than theirs, and thy Employer is faithful to pay thee the reward of thy work."

The Elements of Style

by William Strunk, Jr. & E. B. White
Recommended by: Richard M. Furland,
Chairman & CEO, Squibb Corporation

This book is less than 100 pages long, but a reader who takes its lessons to heart will learn to write elegantly and concisely. For a would-be leader, this is an invaluable skill:

". . . when a sentence is made stronger, it usually becomes shorter. Thus, brevity is a byproduct of vigor."

"Consciously or unconsciously, the reader is dissatisfied with being told only what is not; he wishes to be told what is. Hence, as a rule, it is better to express even a negative in a positive form."

"Every writer, by the way he uses the language, reveals something of his spirit, his habits, his capacities, his bias. This is inevitable, as well as enjoyable. All writing is communication through revelation — it is the Self escaping into the open. No writer long remains incognito."

"Avoid the elaborate, the pretentious, the coy, and the cute. Do not be tempted by a twenty-dollar word when there is a ten-center handy, ready and able."

"The whole duty of a writer is to please and satisfy himself, and the true writer always plays to an audience of one."

Chief Executive Officers

Anthology of Joseph Conrad

by Joseph Conrad
Recommended by: Frank E. Masland, Jr.,
CEO, C. H. Masland & Sons

I have recently been reading an anthology of Joseph Conrad's writings. I ran across a paragraph therein that I thought applied just as well to the world in which we live: "The new hand aboard asked old Singleton who had shipped over 'what kind of ship is this? Eh?' Old Singleton didn't stir a long while, then he said, 'Ship! . . . Ships are all right. It's the men in them.'"

Whale of a Territory

Recommended by: Michael G. O'Neil,
CEO, General Tire & Rubber Co.

As a Man Thinketh

by James Allen
Recommended by: Orson Clay,
CEO, American National Insurance

Essays

by Michel de Montaigne
Recommended by: John Gardner,
Educator, Founder of Common Cause

The essays of Montaigne reached me early when I was about twenty or twenty-one and had the most widening effect, broadening effect, stimulating effect.

To understate the thing, what someone called the "burden of the past" rested very lightly on the shoulders of Californians who grew up in my era. We were not surrounded by an atmosphere of history; the present was very real. The future was almost more real. We just didn't pay much attention to history.

I was not uninformed on the subject, but I still lacked a sense of the past and for me, Montaigne opened that door. A lot of people get their strongest sense of the past from things that are curious, that are quaint, that have an antique flavor. To me, Montaigne brought the past alive for just the opposite reasons. He seemed so contemporary—a sixteenth century Frenchman who spoke to me as though he were a wise contemporary. It was a revelation that a span of four hundred years could make so little difference.

He said, "We're born to search after truth, but not to find it, necessarily. To possess it belongs to a greater power. The question is not who shall win but who shall run the best course." That's the theme that's run over and over again in my own writing, and I haven't any doubt but my introduction to it was Montaigne.

He that I am reading seems always to have the most force.

— Montaigne

Thoughts About Education

According to the order of nature, men being equal, their common vocation is the profession of humanity; and whoever is well educated to discharge the duty of a man cannot be badly prepared to fill any of those offices that have a relation to him. It matters little to me whether my pupil be designed for the army, the pulpit, or the bar of justice. Nature has destined us to the offices of human life antecedent to our destination concerning society. To live is the profession I would teach him. When I have done with him, it is true he will be neither a soldier, a lawyer, nor a divine. *Let him first be a man*; Fortune may remove him from one rank to another as she pleases, he will be always found in his place.

—Jean Jacques Rousseau

One barrier that has helped to hold back the happiness that ought to sweep over our land like an advancing flood is found in modern literature. Man's mental mood should reflect the books and philosophy he reads. If former generations were happy in their garrets it was because their favorite authors were optimists, who saw life's good, indeed, yet also saw that evil, in its heart, was also good. The great authors, from Homer and Paul down to Shakespeare, have been the children of exultant joy as well as genius; all were large-natured, sweet, wholesome, healthy, and happy.

—Newell Dwight Hillis

Educators

Ethics

by Aristotle
Recommended by: Mortimer Adler,
Philosopher, Director, Institute for
Philosophical Research, University of Chicago

Aristotle believed that a man who has difficulty behaving ethically is morally imperfect, that moral virtue is a matter of avoiding extremes in behavior. I understood through that book and no other what it means to say we're engaged in the pursuit of happiness.

·Middlemarch

by George Eliot; and

The Moviegoer

by Walker Percy
Recommended by: Robert Coles,
Dept. of Psychiatry, Harvard University

George Eliot's *Middlemarch* is the wisest novel I know. *The Moviegoer* is the wisest novel by a contemporary American novelist.

Structure of Scientific Revolution

by Thomas S. Kuhn
Recommended by: George Lodge
Harvard School of Business

The Selling Process:
A Handbook of Salesmanship

by Norval Hawkins
Recommended by: Harold Geneen,
Former CEO, ITT

I was assigned to a territory on the outer reaches of the city in Queens. I made my rounds by subway and on foot. I remember well my first stop to sell a real estate ad to a big advertiser in Jackson Heights. I had walked a long way to reach him. I hesitated a long while before entering his office, fear in my gut. But I walked in, drew a deep breath, and blurted out, "Would you like to take out some classified this week in the new *World-Telegram*? 'No!'" he shouted at me.

"Thank you very much," said I, beating a hasty retreat, thankful that the ordeal was over.

As I walked back to the subway, it did not take much imagination to realize that that was no way to sell advertising. So I picked up a book on the tactics of selling which said:

Never make your sales pitch right away.

Listen to what he says. Don't interrupt him.

Pick out his main objection and focus on that.

Finally, don't forget to ask for the order.

Another book on selling was far more important to me, for it has guided me in business far beyond the aspects of salesmanship. Written in 1918 by Norval Hawkins, the first sales manager of the Ford Motor Company, it was called *The Selling Process: A Handbook of Salesmanship*. It made a lasting impression upon me. To be a good salesman, essentially, you had to be a good man. It was not the clothes or the sales pitch which made one a good salesman; it was the man himself who gained the confidence of the customer. Hawkins said that a successful salesman had to be as clean as a hound's tooth in body, mind and spirit. He had to be honest and straight.

The True Believer

by Eric Hoffer
Recommended by: Georgie Anne Geyer,
Universal Press Syndicate

The True Believer, because it cuts across so much nonsense to analyze man and his passions as they are.

"Those who would transform a nation or the world cannot do so by breeding and captaining discontent or by demonstrating the reasonableness and desirability of the intended changes or by coercing people into a new way of life. They must know how to kindle and fan an extravagant hope. It matters not whether it be hope of a heavenly kingdom, of heaven on earth, of plunder and untold riches, of fabulous achievement or world dominion. If the Communists win Europe and a large part of the world, it will not be because they know how to stir up discontent or how to infect people with hatred, but because they know how to preach hope.

"The men who started the French Revolution were wholly without political experience. The same is true of the Bolsheviks, Nazis and the revolutionaries in Asia. The experienced man of affairs is a latecomer. He enters the movement when it is already a going concern. It is perhaps the Englishman's political experience that keeps him shy of mass movements."

The proper study of mankind is books.
—Aldous Huxley

Modern Times

by Paul Johnson
Recommended by: Newt Gingrich,
Member of Congress, Georgia

I would recommend *Modern Times*, by Paul Johnson. It is masterful.

"What looked antiquated, even risible, in the 1980s was not religious belief but the confident predictions of its demise once provided by Feuerbach, Marx and Comte, Durkheim and Frazer, Wells, Shaw, Gide and Sartre and countless others. By the end of our period even the term 'secularization' was in disrepute. 'The whole concept appears a tool of counter-religious ideologies,' wrote one professor of sociology angrily, 'which identify the "real" element in religion for polemical purposes and then arbitrarily relate it to the notion of a unitary and irreversible process. . . . [It] should be erased from the sociological vocabulary.' The Secularist movement, that is militant atheism, appears to have peaked in the 1880s, at exactly the same time as its great revival, Protestant Nonconformity, so that Lenin was a survivor rather than a precursor. By the 1980's the museums of anti-God and Chairs of Scientific Atheism he founded were mere historical curiosities. The alternatives to religion, such as Positivism, had vanished almost without trace, confirming John Henry Newman's observation: 'True religion is slow in growth and, when once planted, is difficult of dislogement; but its intellectual counterfeit has no root in itself; it springs up suddenly, it suddenly withers.' It is likely that there were fewer atheists, as such, in 1980 than in 1880."

United States Congressmen

Road to Serfdom
by Friedrich A. Von Hayek

The Conservative Mind
by Russell Kirk
Recommended by: Philip Crane,
Member of Congress, Illinois

It's a toss-up for me. I have two books that I recommend almost hand-in-hand. The first, *The Road to Serfdom*, was written by Friedrich Von Hayek. My other favorite was by Russell Kirk, entitled *The Conservative Mind*.

The Way the World Works
by Jude Wanniski
Recommended by: Jack Kemp,
Member of Congress, New York

Wisdom is wealth, and every good book is equivalent to a wise head — the head may die, but the book may live forever.
— Joseph Wheeler
Member of Congress, Alabama, 1881

United States Senators

Case Book of Sherlock Holmes
by Arthur Conan Doyle
Recommended by: Rudy Boschwitz,
Senator, Minnesota

Victory
by Joseph Conrad
Recommended by: Bill Bradley,
Senator, New Jersey

The Republic
by Plato
Recommended by: Jeremiah Denton,
Senator, Alabama

Lincoln
by Carl Sandburg
Recommended by: Bob Dole,
Senator, Kansas

United States Senators

The Secret Kingdom

by Pat Robertson
Recommended by: Roger Jepsen,
Senator, Iowa

All of Mark Twain's Works

by Mark Twain
Recommended by: Paul Laxalt,
Senator, Nevada

The White Nile

by Alan Moorehead
Recommended by: Ted Stevens,
Senator, Alaska

In a very real sense, people who have read good literature have lived more than people who cannot or will not read . . . It is not true that we have only one life to live; if we can read, we can live as many more lives and as many kinds of lives as we wish.

      − S. I. Hayakawa
       Senator, California

United States Senators

Witness

by Whittaker Chambers
Recommended by: John P. East,
Senator, North Carolina

Tom Swift Adventure Books

by Victor Appleton
Recommended by: John Glenn,
Senator, Ohio

Brothers Karamazov

by Fyodor Dostoyevsky
Recommended by: Orrin Hatch,
Senator, Utah

Profiles in Courage

by John Kennedy
Recommended by: Ernest Hollings,
Senator, South Carolina

Raintree County

by Ross Lockridge
Recommended by: William Glasser, M.D.,
President, William Glasser, Inc.

While my favorite author is Thomas Hardy, and his small book, *The Woodlanders*, is very close to perfect, I think that my one favorite book is *Raintree County*, by Ross Lockridge. More than any other book, it best describes our country, its great virtues and its many faults, through the eyes of as interesting a cast of characters—heroes and scoundrels, con men and crusaders, lovers and exploiters, statesmen and "politicians"—that have ever been assembled in an American novel. If I were to select a book to teach anyone about America, what it has been and what it could be, I would say read this compassionate book. I have read it seven times and it never seems the same. As I mature, the book has "matured" with me and each reading has given me new understanding into that wonderful group of peculiar people whom I feel so much a part of— Americans.

It is chiefly through books that we enjoy intercourse with superior minds. . . . In the best books, great men talk to us, give us their most precious thoughts, and pour their souls into ours.
—William Ellery Channing, *On Self-Culture*

Actualization

by Stewart Emery
Recommended by: Bill Gove, CPAE,
Past President, National Speakers Association

The fundamental nature of the Universe is one of balance and harmony in relationships. There is no separation – you can't make it alone. We not only need others – we are others.

You and I have within us the creative intelligence to recognize the conditions of existence that support our growth toward "self-actualization," and we have the wherewithal to place ourselves in such an environment.

To a person who undergoes transformation, the world is exactly the way it was before. What is altered is the way he feels about it. What is altered is his relationship to the things in his life . . . not the things themselves. He doesn't have to change the world. Just the way he looks at it.

You have inside of you, all you need to become all you want to be. That which you want to be, you probably already are. That which you want to achieve is already in process.

Goals have been a rip-off. Even though we often see them as a solution to making a life, they are usually no more than a solution to making a living. All a goal does is alter the circumstances in which you are the way you are. So a goal is nothing more than an excuse for the game. It is not the game.

Life is a series of adjustments. The quality of the adjustment will determine the quality of your life.

You Can Change the World!

by Father James Keller
Recommended by: J. Peter Grace,
CEO, W.R. Grace and Company

My selection would be *You Can Change the World!* by the late Father James Keller M.M., founder of the Christophers. It was published by Halcyon House in Garden City, New York, in 1948.

Through entertaining anecdotes taken from real life, Father Keller provides a hopeful and practical guide to everyday living for people of all faiths. He counsels young people to take a zealous approach to work and career, and to strive to make a difference in the world, no matter what their position in life.

Father Keller also emphasizes the importance of prayer, love of God and fellow man, and a patriotic spirit as tangible ways to fight Communism and the godless. He deeply believed in the worth of each individual, and this belief was the foundation for the Christopher philosophy which says "there's nobody like you," and "you can make a difference." Father Keller's writings have been a guidepost for me throughout my personal and professional life.

God be thanked for books. They are the voices of the distant and the dead, and make us heirs of the spiritual life of past ages.

– Channing

Biography

Of all the species of literary composition perhaps biography is the most delightful. The attention concentrated on one individual gives a unity to the materials of which it is composed, which is wanting in general history. The train of incidents through which it conducts the reader suggests to his imagination a multitude of analogies and comparisons; and while he is following the course of events which mark the life of him who is the subject of the narrative, he is insensibly compelled to take a retrospect of his own. In no other species of writing are we permitted to scrutinize the character so exactly, or to form so just and accurate an estimate of the excellences and defects, the lights and shades, the blemishes and beauties, of an individual mind.

– Robert Hall

Read no history, nothing but biography, for that is life without theory.

– Benjamin Disraeli

Of all studies, the most delightful and the most useful is biography. The seeds of great events lie near the surface; historians delve too deep for them. No history was ever true. Lives I have read which, if they were not, had the appearance, the interest, and the utility of truth.

– Landor

The Book

Heine and The Book

What a book! Great and wide as the world, rooted in the abysmal depths of creation and rising aloft into the blue mysteries of heaven . . . Sunrise and sunset, promise and fulfilment, birth and death, the whole human drama, everything is in the book. . . . It is the book of books.

1840

The Bible, that great medicine chest of humanity.

1844

I owe my enlightenment entirely to an old, simple book, as plain and modest as nature itself . . . a book as weekday like and unpretending as the sun which warms us or the bread which nourishes us; a book which greets us with all the intimate confidence, blessed affection and kind glance of an old grandmother. . . . This is called with cause the Holy Scripture. He who lost his God may find Him again in this book, and he who has never known Him will inhale here the breath of God's word. The Jews who are connoisseurs of valuables, knew very well what they were about when, in the conflagration of the Second Temple, they left the gold and silver vessels of sacrifice, the candelabra and lamps, even the High Priest's breastplate with its large jewels, and rescued only the Bible. This was the real treasure of the Temple.

1852

The Jews . . . trudged around with it all through the Middle Ages as with a portable fatherland.

1854

Milton and The Book

The Scripture affords us a divine pastoral drama in the Song of Solomon, consisting of two persons and a double chorus, as Origen rightly judges; and the Apocalypse of St. John is a majestic image of a high and stately tragedy, shutting and intermingling her solemn scenes and acts with a sevenfold chorus of hallelujahs and harping symphonies. And this my opinion, the grave authority of Pareus, commenting that book, is sufficient to confirm. Or, if occasion shall lead, to imitate those magnific odes and hymns, wherein Pindarus and Callimachus are in most things worthy, some others in their frame judicious, in their matter most an end faulty. But those frequent songs, throughout the laws and prophets, beyond all these, not in their divine argument alone, but in the very original art of composition, may be easily made appear over all the kinds of lyric poesy to be incomparable.

It is not hard for any man who hath a Bible in his hands, to borrow good words and holy sayings in abundance; but to make them his own is a work of grace only from above.

There are no songs comparable to the songs of Zion; no orations equal to those of the Prophets; and no politics like those which the Scriptures teach.

The Book of Life
A Treasure of Wisdom

The book of Life is the tabernacle wherein the treasure of wisdom is to be found. The truth of voice perishes with the sound; truth latent in the mind is hidden wisdom and invisible treasure; but the truth which illuminates books desires to manifest itself to every disciplinable sense. Let us consider how great a commodity of doctrine exists in books, – how easily, how secretly, how safely, they expose the nakedness of human ignorance without putting it to shame. These are the masters that instruct us without rods and ferules, without hard words and anger, without clothes or money. If you approach them, they are not asleep; if, investigating, you interrogate them, they conceal nothing; if you mistake them, they never grumble; if you are ignorant, they cannot laugh at you.

– Richard de Bury, *Philobiblon*, 1344

Book of Job

I call the Book of Job apart from all theories about it, one of the grandest things ever written with pen. One feels, indeed, as if it were not Hebrew; such a noble universality, different from noble patriotism, or sectarianism, reigns in it. A noble book! All men's book! It is our first, oldest statement of the never-ending problem, man's destiny, and God's ways with him here in this earth. And all in such free flowing outlines; grand in its sincerity, in its simplicity, in its epic melody and repose of reconcilement. There is the seeing eye, the mildly understanding heart. So true every way; true eyesight and vision for all things; material things no less than spiritual: the horse, – "Hast thou clothed his neck with *thunder?*" "he *laughs* at the shaking of the spear!" Such living likenesses were never since drawn. Sublime sorrow, sublime reconciliation; oldest choral melody as of the heart of mankind; so soft and great; as the summer midnight, as the world with its seas and stars! There is nothing written, I think, in the Bible or out of it, of equal literary merit.

– Carlyle

Greats on The Book

It is our duty to live among books; especially to live by one book, and a very old one.
—John Henry Newman, *Tracts for the Times*.

I am a man of one book.
St. Thomas Aquinas, referring to the fact that he read only the Bible.
Aquinas was once asked, with what compendium a man might become learned. He answered, "By reading of one book."

All systems of morality are fine. The Gospel alone has exhibited a complete assemblage of the principles of morality, divested of all absurdity. It is not composed, like your creed, of a few commonplace sentences put into bad verse. Do you wish to see that which is really sublime? Repeat the Lord's Prayer.
—Napoleon I

The Bible begins gloriously with Paradise, the symbol of youth, and ends with the everlasting kingdom, with the holy city. The history of every man should be a Bible.

—Novalis

Greats on The Book

The translators of the Bible were masters of an English style much fitter for that work than any we see in our present writings; the which is owing to the simplicity that runs through the whole.

— Swift

My own experience is that the Bible is dull when I am dull. When I am really alive, and set in upon the text with a tidal pressure of living affinities, it opens, it multiplies discoveries, and reveals depths even faster than I can note them. The worldly spirit shuts the Bible; the Spirit of God makes it a fire, flaming out all meanings and glorious truths.

— Horace Bushnell

The general diffusion of the Bible is the most effectual way to civilize and humanize mankind; to purify and exalt the general system of public morals; to give efficacy to the just precepts of international and municipal law; to enforce the observance of prudence, temperance, justice, and fortitude; and to improve all the relations of social and domestic life.

— Chancellor Kent

Presidents and The Book

It is impossible to govern the world without God and the Bible.

—George Washington

So great is my veneration of the Bible that the earlier my children begin to read it the more confident will be my hope that they will prove useful citizens of their country and respectable members of society.

—John Quincy Adams

The whole inspiration of our civilization springs from the teachings of Christ and the lessons of the prophets. To read the Bible for these fundamentals is a necessity of American life.

—Herbert Hoover

"In regard to this great book, I have but to say, it is the best gift God has given to man. All the good Savior gave to the world was communicated through this book. But for it we could not know right from wrong. All things most desirable for man's welfare, here and hereafter, are to be found portrayed in it."

—Abraham Lincoln

Presidents and The Book

"Every thinking man, when he thinks, realises that the teachings of the Bible are so interwoven and entwined with our whole civic and social life that it would be literally impossible for us to figure ourselves what that life would be if these standards were removed. We would lose almost all the standards by which we now judge both public and private morals; all the standards towards which we, with more or less resolution, strive to raise ourselves."

–Theodore Roosevelt

"A man had deprived himself of the best there is in the world who has deprived himself of this, a knowledge of the Bible. When you have read the Bible, you will know that it is the Word of God, because you will have found it the key to your own heart, your own happiness, and your own duty."

–Woodrow Wilson

"Hold fast to the Bible as the sheet-anchor of your liberties; write its precepts in your hearts and practice them in your lives. To the influence of this book we are indebted for all the progress made in true civilization, and to this we must look as our guide in the future. 'Righteousness exalteth a nation; but sin is a reproach to any people.'"

– U. S. Grant

Greats on The Book

I find more sure marks of the authenticity of the Bible than in any profane history whatever. . . . Worshipping God and the Lamb in the temple: God, for his benefaction in creating all things, and the Lamb, for his benefaction in redeeming us with his blood.

—Sir Isaac Newton

The history I am going to speak of is that of Joseph in Holy Writ, which is related with such majestic simplicity, that all the parts of it strike us with strong touches of nature and compassion; and he must be a stranger to both, who can read it with attention and not be overwhelmed wth the vicissitudes of joy and sorrow. I hope it will not be a profanation to tell it one's own way here, that they who may be unthinking enough to be more frequently readers of such papers as this, than of Sacred Writ, may be advertised that the greatest pleasures the imagination can be entertained with are to be found there, and that even the style of the Scriptures is more than heaven.

—Sir R. Steele, *Tatler*, No. 233

Greats on The Book

The most learned, acute, and diligent student cannot, in the longest life, obtain an entire knowledge of this one volume. The more deeply he works the mine, the richer and more abundant he finds the ore; new light continually beams from this source of heavenly knowledge, to direct the conduct, and illustrate the work of God and the ways of men; and he will at last leave the world confessing that the more he studied the Scriptures, the fuller conviction he had of his *own ignorance*, and of *their inestimable value*.

— Sir Walter Scott

I have carefully and regularly perused these Holy Scriptures, and am of opinion that the volume, independently of its divine origin, contains more true sublimity, more exquisite beauty, purer morality, more important history, and finer strains of poetry and eloquence, than could be collected within the same compass from all other books, in whatever age or language they may have been written.

— Sir William Jones

Wernher Von Braun & The Book

"How do you then see the Bible in this day and age?" He was asked.

"The two things that Immanuel Kant admired so much – 'The starry sky above me and the moral law within me' – truly represent the same reality," he replied.

"In this age of space flight, when we use the modern tools of science to advance into new regions of human activity, the Bible – this grandiose, stirring history of the gradual revelation and unfolding of the moral law – remains in every way an up-to-date book. Our knowledge and use of the laws of nature that enable us to fly to the Moon also enable us to destroy our home planet with the atom bomb. Science itself does not address the question whether we should use the power at our disposal for good or for evil. The guidelines of what we ought to do are furnished in the moral law of God. It is no longer enough that we pray that God may be with us on our side. We must learn again to pray that we may be on God's side."

Fulton John Sheen
The Book of Life

Carlyle was wrong in saying that "there is no life of a man faithfully recorded." Mine was! The ink used was blood, the parchment was skin, the pen was a spear. Over eight chapters make up the book, each for a year of my life. Though I pick it up every day, it never reads the same. The more I lift my eyes from its pages, the more I feel the need of doing my own autobiography that all might see what I want them to see. But the more I fasten my gaze on it, the more I see that everything worthwhile in it was received as a gift from Heaven. Why then should I glory in it?

That old autobiographical volume was like the sun. The farther I walked from it, the deeper and the longer were the shadows that stretched before my eyes: regrets, remorse and fears. But as I walked toward it, the shadows fell behind me, less awesome but still reminders of what I had left undone. But when I took the book into my hands, there were no shadows either fore or aft, but the supernal joy of being bathed in light. It was like walking directly under the sun, no mirages to solicit, no phantoms to follow.

That autobiography is the crucifix – the inside story of my life not in the way it walks the stage of time, but how it was recorded, taped and written in the Book of Life.

The Miracle Book

"This miracle book has been the source of the inspiration which has stirred our great pioneers to the achievements and discoveries of past days.

Sir Christopher Wren in Architecture

Sir Isaac Newton in Science

Robert Boyle who devised the barometer

Michael Faraday, the pioneer in Electricity

William Haskell, the Astronomer

William Harvey, who discovered the
circulation of blood

James Y. Simpson, the discoverer of Anaesthetics

Lord Kelvin famous in Physics

John Howard in Prison Reform

William Wilberforce in Slavery Abolition

Florence Nightingale in Nursing

Lord Shaftesbury, Dr. Barnardo, George Muller,
Willam Quarrier in the rescue of
Downtrodden Children

David Livingstone in Exploration

Cruden of Concordance Fame, and

George Williams, the founder of Y.M.C.A.

—all these and countless others would have testified to have gained the inspiration for their great humanitarian labours from the Bible."

The Book

Prize and study the Scripture. We can have no delight in meditation on him unless we know him; and we cannot know him but by the means of his own revelation; when the revelation is despised, the revealer will be of little esteem. Men do not throw off God from being their rule, till they throw off Scripture from being their guide; and God must needs be cast off from being an end, when the Scripture is rejected from being a rule. Those that do not care to know his will, that love to be ignorant of his nature, can never be affected to his honour. Let therefore the subtleties of reason vail to the doctrine of faith, and the humour of the will to the command of the word.

—Charnock: *Attributes*

The Bible is the Iliad of religion.

—Joseph Joubert

If you are ever tempted to speak lightly or think lightly of it, just sit down and imagine what this world would be without it. No Bible! A wound and no cure, a storm and no covert, a condemnation and no shrift, a lost eternity and no ransom! Alas for us if this were all; alas for us if the ladder of science were the only stair to lead us up to God!

—R. R. Meredith

The All-Purpose Book

"*John Milton* declared that 'there are no songs to be compared to the songs of Zion, no orations to equal those of the Prophets, and no politics equal to those the Scriptures can teach us.' *John Ruskin* said: 'to my early knowledge of the Bible I owe the best part of my taste in literature, and the most precious, and, on the whole, the one essential part of my education.' *Charles Reade* declared that The Book of Jonah is the most beautiful story ever written in so small a compass. *Coleridge* pronounced The Book of Proverbs 'the best statesman manual ever written,' and *Wordsworth*, referring to the same book, called it 'the world's moral and spiritual manual for all time.' *Edwin Everett*, the prince among orators, studied Proverbs to improve his English.

Thomas Carlyle declared The Book of Job to be the greatest poem in the world. *Benjamin Franklin* read The Book of Habakkuk to a literary circle in Paris which had been ridiculing the church and the Bible, and won unqualified admiration for its literary beauty. The Bible, testified *Dr. Richard Garnett*, keeper of the printed books at the British Museum, 'even regarded from a mere literary point of view is inexhaustible, and when the literary charm of the Bible takes hold of the reader, the study of it becomes a duty altogether delightful.'"

Wilbur Smith and Bible Literature

I trust that some of my readers will begin to special-
ize in some one area of Biblical literature. Though it
is a rather expensive project, a collection of books on
the Bible in Art would be most fascinating. Never before have so many notable books on this subject been
issued as in the last ten years. Or, one might begin to
gather different reference Bibles in the English language. Often these can be purchased for a very small
sum, in second-hand bookstores; actually, that is where
most of them will have to be found, for many reference
Bibles are now out-of-print. Undoubtedly the greatest
subject in all the world for consideration, study, and
meditation, is the Person and Work of the Lord Jesus
Christ. I would estimate that there are at least 65,000
different volumes on the life of Christ in the languages
of western Europe! If one should wish to confine oneself
to a single area in this inexhaustible theme, I would
earnestly commend those volumes which relate to our
Lord's holy death, including literature on the Atone-
ment, the Cross, the Seven Last Words, and related sub-
jects.

The Little Black Book

by Marion Wade,
Former Chairman, Service Master Company

"If an executive is sincerely searching for a code of ethics by which to operate his business at the most honorable level, he doesn't have to look far, no farther, in fact, than that *Little Black Book* which is in every hotel room — and which ought to be on every executive's desk. And he must know that he cannot acquire its guidance by osmosis. He must first of all truly believe that the Bible is God talking to him and that it is his Christian duty to do what he is told. He must then read the Bible regularly, daily seeking to understand it in context, and he should realize that though he may read it through many times he will never understand it all but he will nevertheless learn something new each time."

"The Psalmist wrote, 'The word is a lamp unto my feet, and a light unto my path. I have sworn and I will perform it, that I will keep thy righteous judgments. Thy testimonies have I taken as an heritage forever; for they are the rejoicing of my heart. I have inclined mine heart to perform thy statutes always, even unto the end.'" (Psalm 119:105, 106, 111, 112)

A Businessman Looks at the Bible

by W. Maxey Jarman,
former Chairman, Genesco, Inc.

"The Bible is the best self-help Book in the world, and it can help you reduce your shortcomings. It can throw light on your weaknesses and faults and show you how to do something about them. Of course, if you begin to concentrate on your own faults, you won't have the time or inclination to look for them in someone else, so that is an added benefit. To those who seem to enjoy critizing others and complaining about the world—which is neither the route to popularity nor very healthy—I would also recommend the Bible, for it would give them a new outlook on life.

"There are days in every life when things do not look bright, when it is easy to become discouraged, and when even our best efforts do not produce good results. These are the times to seek help from the Bible. If you read it regularly, it will give you a new outlook, an encouraging uplift, a boost for your morale, and you will know fewer periods of depression.

"As long as we are in the flesh and in this dispensation, none of us is going to be absolutely sinless, but that doesn't mean that we should give way to vice. It is our job to fight against the weakness of the flesh, but we don't get very far on our own strength."

"Worry Clinic" – Feb. 27, 1984
A daily syndicated column
by George W. Crane, Ph.D., M.D.

My contribution will show why I gained more practical ideas from the Bible than from college!

GREATEST BOOK

As both a teaching university psychologist and also a psychiatrist, I spent 12 years of undergraduate and graduate study at Yale and Northwestern University to gain my Ph.D. and M.D.

But I gleaned more practical psychology and psychiatry from the Bible, than from all other books!

It shows us the first and most widely used invention of mankind, namely, passing the buck.

For Adam got out of a dilemma when God accused him of eating the forbidden fruit, as by saying:

"The woman whom thou gavest to me for a wife, she gave it to me."

God then turned to criticize Eve, but she saw how neatly Adam had passed the buck to her, so she did the same thing for the serpent.

Incidentally, the serpent was the original star salesman who sold Eve, not Adam, for salesman prefer women customers, since they are more gifted with words and enjoy language far more than men.

The Bible also shows that God enjoys people who can talk easily (and also write interesting copy) for when Moses tried to beg off from facing Pharaoh by telling God "I am a man slow of speech," God's anger was kindled against Moses.

But God compromised and paid mankind the first spoken compliment by telling Moses to let his brother Aaron be his "mouthpiece" saying:

"I know that he can speak well!"

God also enjoys people who can argue deftly, as when Abraham bartered with God, asking if Sodom would be spared if 50 righteous people were therein, and God agreed.

Then Abraham lowered the number to 45, then 40, 30, 20 and even 10 and God still assented, but only 4 escaped Sodom's fire & brimstone!

Moses also persuaded God at the time of the Golden Calf episode, for God then vowed he was through with the Israelites and would wipe them all out but make a new nation just of Moses and his own children.

But Moses used super salesmanship and God relented.

King Hezekiah also uttered a logical prayer that caused God to cure him and add 15 more years to his lifespan, so God relishes salesmen!

John Bunyan and The Book

Author of Pilgrim's Progress

For twelve years Bunyan was kept in the County Jail of Bedford: but the iron gates could not shut out the rich compensations of God. . . . He had few books apart from the Bible, but he soon made himself master of God's message of Grace; and the truth which he found in the Bible was applied and tested in the experience of his own heart. "I never had in all my life so great an inlet into the Word of God as now," he wrote; ". . . Jesus Christ also was never more real . . . than now: here I have seen Him and felt Him indeed." Bunyan had not much to offer in the way of human learning and would not place himself in debt even for a thread or a shoe-lachet to the scholars of his own age; yet he arrived at a remarkable knowledge of Truth by his study of the Scriptures with much prayer and meditation. "Expositors I reverence, but must live by mine own faith," he wrote; "God hath nowhere bound Himself to them more than to others with respect to the revelation of His mind in His Word." "I honour the godly as Christians," he said, "but I prefer the Bible before them; and having that still with me, I count myself far better furnished than if I had without it all the libraries of the two Universities. Besides I am for drinking water out of my own cistern; what God makes mine by the evidence of His Word and Spirit, that I dare make bold with." This close study of the Bible furnished him with a store of things both new and old with which his own writings were to shine and sparkle.

– Marcus L. Loane

C. S. Lewis on St. Paul

St. Paul is the Christian author whom no one can by-pass.

A most astonishing misconception has long dominated the modern mind on the subject of St. Paul. It is to this effect: that Jesus preached a kindly and simple religion (found in the Gospels) and that St. Paul afterwards corrupted it into a cruel and complicated religion (found in the Epistles). This is really quite untenable. All the most terrifying texts come from the mouth of Our Lord: all the texts on which we can base such warrant as we have for hoping that all men will be saved come from St. Paul. If it could be proved that St. Paul altered the teaching of his Master in any way, he altered it in exactly the opposite way to that which is popularly supposed. But there is no real evidence for a pre-Pauline doctrine different from St. Paul's. The Epistles are, for the most part the earliest Christian documents we possess. The Gospels come later.

. . . The nineteenth-century attack on St. Paul was really only a stage in the revolt against Christ. Men were not ready in any large numbers to attack Christ Himself. They made the normal first move – that of attacking one of His principal ministers. Everything they disliked in Christianity was therefore attributed to St. Paul. It was unfortunate that their case could not impress anyone who had really read the Gospels and the Epistles with attention: but apparently few people had and so the first victory was won.

–God in the Dock, 1970

George Washington Carver
and
"An Old Book"

George Washington Carver has been called the world's greatest biochemist. By discovering hundreds of valuable uses for the peanut and sweet potato, he revolutionized Southern agriculture and rose to such prominence that Thomas A. Edison offered him a position at a salary running into six figures. In 1921, Dr. Carver was invited to testify before the Senate Ways and Means Committee on the possibilities of the peanut. Given ten minutes to speak, he so enthralled the committee that the chairman said, "Go ahead Brother. Your time is unlimited." Carver talked for one hour and forty-five minutes, long past time for adjournment. At the conclusion of his address the chairman asked, "Dr. Carver, how did you learn all of these things?" Carver replied, "From AN OLD BOOK." "What book?" the Senator inquired. Then came the great man's significant answer: "The Bible."

"Does the Bible tell about peanuts?" the surprised Senator queried. "No, sir," Dr. Carver replied, "but it tells about the God who made the peanut. I asked Him to show me what to do with the peanut, and He did."

Carl Sandburg and The Book

One of my most vivid early memories is our first home Bible, a small Swedish-language Bible. I was about four years old and it was in the Berrien Street house, in the second-floor bedroom of my father and mother. It was winter, with winds howling outside. Mary and I heard father read a chapter by the light of a small kerosene lamp. Several times that week I went to where the Book lay on top of a bureau, and I opened it and turned the pages. I asked my mother to point out certain words I remembered. I took comfort in mother saying it would be clear to me whenI started school and learned to read.

Mark Twain and Moses

There are those who deny the existence of Moses, just as there are those who deny the existence of Homer, of Shakespeare, of Jesus. Unable to explain the *great* men of the world, the *little* men of the world try to explain them away. But Mark Twain with his logical humor has disposed of all these cynics who doubt the reality of Moses. "If the Ten Commandments were not written by Moses," observes Mark Twain, "then they were written by another fellow of the same name." And Heine, with equal humor and with even greater logic remarks that if Moses was not created by God, then the writers of the *Old Testament* did well to remind God of His oversight by creating Moses themselves. For the early Hebrews needed an extraordinary type of prophet to weld them into a living nation under the leadership of God. And the one prophet who succeeded in doing this was Moses.

—Henry and Dana Thomas, 1942

Napoleon I and The Book

The Gospel possesses a secret virtue, a mysterious efficacy, a warmth which penetrates and soothes the heart. One finds in meditating upon it that which one experiences in contemplating the heavens. The Gospel is not a book; it is a living being, with an action, a power, which invades everything that opposes its extension. Behold it upon this table, this book surpassing all others (here the Emperor solemnly placed his hand upon it): I never omit to read it, and every day with the same pleasure. . . . Not only is our mind absorbed, it is controlled; and the soul can never go astray with this book for its guide. Once master of our spirit, the faithful Gospel loves us. God even is our friend, our father, and truly our God. The mother has no greater care for the infant whom she nurses.

What a proof of the divinity of Christ! With an empire so absolute, he has but one single end, — the spiritual melioration of individuals, the purity of conscience, the union to that which is true, the holiness of the soul. . . . If you [General Bertrand] do not perceive that Jesus Christ is God, very well: then I did wrong to make you a general.

— Napoleon I (at St. Helena)

A Book
I'd Like
To Share

In Search of Excellence

by Thomas Peters and Robert Waterman, Jr.
Recommended by: K. J. Griggy,
CEO, Wilson Foods Corporation

While picking one book is difficult, my choice of
the book I have profited most from recently is *In
Search of Excellence,* by Thomas Peters and Robert
Waterman, Jr.

Management excellence is a continuing quest in
American industry. *In Search of Excellence* does a superb
job relating the basics of excellence to the constantly
changing world of today. The eight attributes of excellence that innovative companies offer any businessman, in any business, are an important yardstick by
which to direct and measure performance. Progress
toward excellence in an age of turbulent change must
be predicated on a few basics. *In Search of Excellence*
focuses on these basics and provides a set of values
which are ageless.

"'Leadership over human beings is exercised when
persons with certain motives and purposes mobilize,
in competition or conflict with others, institutional,
political, psychological and other resources so as to
arouse, engage and satisfy the motives of followers.' In
essence, Burns says, 'Leadership, unlike naked power
wielding, is thus inseparable from followers' needs and
goals.' He thereby sets the stage for a concise defini-
tion of transforming leadership."

The Patton Principles

by Porter B. Williamson
Recommended by: Bruce C. Hagen,
B.A.S., D.C.

One of the most thought provoking and life influenc-
ing books that I have ever read is *The Patton Principles*.
General Patton was America's most successful general
during World War II. This fiesty, outspoken, two-fisted,
revolver-toting, immaculately dressed, profane, and
religious general never lost a battle during World War II.

When General Patton took command of the defeated
troops in Africa, the first thing he did was make the
soldiers shave, wear clean and pressed uniforms, and
order them to be properly attired at all times. A soldier with a poor self-image was no good to either his
country or himself.

Although General Patton was an outspoken critic of
the foreign leaders and his superior officers and was
badly maligned for his slapping incident of a battle-
fatigued soldier, he did much to shorten and win World
War II. Had he been turned loose to pursue his destiny,
World War II may have been shortened even more and
millions of lives may have been saved. When German
units found out that they were going to fight Patton's
army, they threw down their arms and surrendered.

Patton was portrayed as one who believed in reincarnation. He was not a believer in reincarnation. He was
such a good militaristic scholar that he knew the battlefield intimately from his study of history.

Enthusiasm Makes The Difference

by Norman Vincent Peale
Recommended by: Ken Hatfield,
Football Coach, University of Arkansas

I would whole-heartedly recommend *Enthusiasm Makes the Difference*, by Norman Vincent Peale. I have used excerpts from it many times to share with others in hope that they can keep a positive feeling that never runs out. Emotions run up and down, but enthusiasm can be constant. I appreciate the positive enforcement the book gave me and its specific guidelines for different types of situations.

The book also has practical applications for anybody with a Christian background. I appreciated that.

"Enthusiasm – the priceless quality that makes everything different! – that is the message of this book."

"Life is not all sweetness and light, not by a great deal; certainly not with its manifold difficulty, pain, and frustration. This book faces life exactly as it is. But, a creative solution is offered – a solution that works. This is an in-spite-of type of book. In spite of all the negatives you can bring forth the positives."

"Interest, excitement, aliveness – that is what this book is about."

"It shows that you need not have a dull, routinized, desultory existence – not at all! Never settle for such a thing. And regardless of harsh, painful, and discouraging situations you can be alive, vital, and on top of things."

How to Win Over Worry

by John Haggai
Recommended by: Bob Hawkins, Sr.,
President, Harvest House Publishers

This book I found to be one of the most enlightening and helpful books I had ever read. I've read it several times since and intend to read it again within the next few months.

Most of us are not immune from worry, including myself. This book is very helpful and soothing. It clearly shows how we can improve our daily living by conquering worry.

"Remember the formula: Praise Plus Poise Plus Prayer Equals Peace. Write this formula in large letters. Place one on the mirror of your medicine cabinet where you shave or on the mirror of your dresser. It will be well for the husband to place one in a conspicuous place in the office where he works and for the housewife to have one placed over the sink or in some prominent place where it will catch her eye during the daytime. It will also be well if you will attach one to the sun-visor in your automobile. You will find great profit if you will place this formula in several conspicuous places where it will command your attention several times during the day.

"Let me further suggest that you memorize the verses found in Philippians 4:4–8. It will be helpful for you to repeat them aloud every morning and every night until they become a part of you."

Stronger Than Steel

by R. C. Sproul
Recommended by: Bill Hayes,
President, National Merchandising Corp.

Why not?

That's the attitude of Wayne Alderson when he talks about his succesful labor-management concept called "Value of the Person" or "Theory R," where both management and labor treat each other with respect, dignity and love.

Wayne Alderson is from the coal fields of Pennsylvania. He has been through all the problems that the coal fields can inflict. He saw his father die and his family evicted from company housing. After that, their only shelter was a tent.

He fought the Germans in World War II and was severely wounded while a point man in the infantry, saved only by a buddy who shielded his body from enemy fire. He went to college, got into management, and was the catalyst that ended a bitter 83-day strike at Pittron Steel.

Because of the tremendous hate, disrespect, and indignities shown the foundry workers, Wayne Alderson's "Value of the Person" concept was like turning on the light in a dark room.

Within 21 months a nearly bankrupt business became profitable.

A few of the simple truths that Wayne Alderson used in his leadership were, "Respect a man's family and you respect the man," "Value a man and he will value his work," and, "Value his work and you will value his ideas." The concept is so simple that it's radical, but it works.

Compensation

by Ralph Waldo Emerson
Recommended by: Woody Hayes,
Football coach emeritus, Ohio State University

There are always two sides, always the other side of the coin. For every good thing there's a bad one; for all lightness, there's dark. When you start looking at anything you do, you must consider the consequences. For example:

In coaching big-time football, I never got into any scandals, I never had any big problems with youngsters because of one thing: I was going to wring all the football from them I could get, and I did. (We had more All-Americans than anybody else.) We're going to get all the football out of the youngster, but what is he going to get in return?

What he'll get in return is the opportunity for the best education he can get in college, and the person who can make sure he doesn't shirk that, because lots of kids will overlook that part, the one who can do that better than anyone else is the head football coach.

There's been no football coach in this country who's spent more time at the study table with his football players than Woody Hayes has. And if Woody Hayes sets the example, the other coaches will follow and the players will be there.

It all comes back to the inevitable question: If you're going to utilize a man, what are you going to give him in return?

If we encountered a man of rare intellect, we should ask him what books he read.

—Emerson

Profiles in Courage

by John F. Kennedy
Recommended by: Leona M. Helmsley,
President, Helmsley Hotels

I was deeply moved by *Profiles in Courage*, both because of the author and the people he wrote about. The fact that John Kennedy used his time in the hospital recovering from a spinal operation to do the work is itself an inspiration and a lesson in personal courage. The book is about people in politics under pressure who didn't go along, but kept true to their personal convictions. John Quincy Adams, Kennedy tells us, "defended his constituents' interests against their delusions." Despite enormous pressure, Edmund G. Ross, an obscure Senator from Kansas, cast the decisive vote to prevent the impeachment of President Andrew Johnson. Both men simply did what they thought was right. Kennedy's book, and life, underscore the eloquence of courage, and show us that the place we all must look for it is within ourselves:

"To be courageous, these stories make clear, requires no exceptional qualifications, no magic formula, no special combination of time, place and circumstance. It is an opportunity that sooner or later is presented to us all. Politics merely furnishes one arena which imposes special tests of courage. In whatever arena of life one may meet the challenge of courage, whatever may be the sacrifices he faces if he follows his conscience — each man must decide for himself the course he will follow."

My Own Story

by Bernard M. Baruch
Recommended by: Major General John W. Hepfer,
U.S.A.F. — Retired

My first encounter with *My Own Story* came in 1957,
the year it was published. My objective in that reading was to learn the basic rules of investing so that I
might supplement my income. While the principles
essential to a sound investment strategy were clearly
in evidence, I found Baruch's philosophy and precepts
of life to be equally interesting and useful. Recalling
his astute observations on people, government and
business, I have returned to the book many times over
the past three decades. Each reading brought renewed
amazement at his insight and ability to foresee the
problems of future generations. This should come as
no surprise when one notes that Baruch, one of the
country's leading financiers, also held many top level
positions in government over a sixty-year span and
was a personal advisor to eight of our Presidents.

One notable characteristic of Baruch evidenced
throughout the book was his great concern for integrity. He continued to fret over some aspersions rela-
tive to his investments which had occurred nearly
fifty years prior to the writing of his story. Another
evidenced characteristic of the author was that he was
a thinker. The book contains some pertinent thoughts
on Why People Work, Understanding Central America,
and Measuring Progress of a Country. He was not a
great writer but he had many great experiences to
include in his writing.

Congressional Medal of Honor Recipients

The Lessons of History

by Will and Ariel Durant
Recommended by: Leo Thorsness,
Six years POW

Without question, my favorite is: *The Lessons of History*, by Will and Ariel Durant.

The older I become, the surer I become that using time to study the past saves time in the future. Not only is time saved by applying past lessons to current problems; face also is saved by not making the same mistakes made by those before us. Forgotten history is repeated history.

New Every Morning

author unknown
Recommended by: James R. Hendrix,
U.S. Army Retired—World War II

Congressional Medal of Honor Recipients

The Making of George Washingtion

by *William H. Wilbur*
Recommended by: William Hall,
Lt. Commander, U.S.N.R.

The Making of George Washington, by William H. Wilbur, should be read by every high school student and by every citizen. It is the best introduction to the integrity of the U.S. of America ever written.

The *23rd Psalm.* A staff of courage and a rod of faith to everyone who knows and worships the true name, our Lord Jesus Christ.

The Three Musketeers — to me a book of courage and inspiration of comradely loyalty, and true friendship; attributes we all need to survive in life before death.

Samuel Johnson

by *W. Jackson Bate*
Recommended by: Michael Daly,
Infantry Captain, U.S. Army

"Books have always a secret influence on the understanding; we cannot at pleasure obliterate ideas: he that reads books of science, though without any desire fixed of improvement, will grow more knowing, he that entertains himself with moral or religious treatises will imperceptibly advance in goodness."

— Samuel Johnson

Congressional Medal of Honor Recipients

Battle Cry

by Leon Uris
Recommended by: Wesley L. Fox,
Lt. Col., U.S. Marine Corps

I guess if you were to hold me to one book, an early book in my life that has helped me to be the Marine that I am today, I would have to name *Battle Cry*.

The value to me was not for any one thought but for the overall tone of what being a Marine is all about. Leon Uris covered very well what our nation expects from its Marines and what those before us have given in the name of "Marine."

The One Minute Father

by Spencer Johnson
Recommended by: Gerald Young,
Lt. Col., U.S. Air Force

The Prophet

by Kahlil Gibran
Recommended by: Pat Brady,
Colonel, U.S. Army

Be My Guest

by Conrad Hilton
Recommended by: Barron Hilton,
CEO, Hilton Hotels

Many people have told me that they were inspired by the message conveyed in my father's autobiography, *Be My Guest*:

"What I like about prayer is that it is a means of communication with God. You can speak to Him any time, night or day, and you can know with certainty that He is listening to you.

"What I like about prayer is that there is no set formula for calling general headquarters on our private walkie-talkie. There are no call letters. You are free to send any message you want. You can just say 'hello'; you can ask for something. You can tell Him that things are going rough and you need reinforcements—as those boys in the jungle did. You can call to thank Him for the things He has done for you. You can tell Him you are baffled, bewildered, discouraged or that you are the happiest person in the world.

"For me, in personal living, in fulfilling our place in the world, in faithful use of our talents, each of these is a spoke in the circle of successful living. Prayer is the hub that holds the wheel together. Without our contact with God we are nothing. With it we are 'a little lower than the angels, crowned with glory and honor.'

"We are successes in the Art of Living."

The Real Race

by Skip Wilkins and Joseph Dunn
Recommended by: Randy Hoffman,
Insurance Executive

Skip Wilkins was on his way to a promising career as a college athlete when he suffered permanent injury in a water-skiing accident. *The Real Race* is the story of Skip Wilkins and his family as they picked up the pieces and built a new life. That new life includes more than 100 medals and an award for the U.S. Athlete of the Year in wheelchair sports. It includes a college education, a job and a loving wife. It includes hope and determination to help others today and a new-found faith about his tomorrows.

"I wasn't accustomed to the demands of the practice sessions. We were up early, pushing long distances to the bus for the ride to the stadium, then sitting throughout the day as the teams worked out.

"The hours of sitting in the chair took their toll. The callus on my rear split open. Before the competition started, I was worn out from the daily routine, I saw Daphne infrequently, the callus was causing me physical and mental problems, and I had seen some of the best conditioned athletes in the world. My sole source of strength flowed from my reading of now familiar Scriptures and frequent prayer.

"I took special refuge in Paul's words in Second Corinthians, when he explains man's weakness in relation to Christ's strength: 'That is why, for Christ's sake, I delight in weaknesses, in insults, in hardships, in persecutions, in difficulties. For when I am weak, then I am strong.'"

The Magic Of Thinking Big

by David Schwartz
Recommended by: Lou Holtz,
Football Coach, University of Minnesota

There are two books that come to my mind instantly that I've enjoyed thoroughly. One is *The Magic Of Thinking Big*, by David Schwartz, and the other one is *See You At The Top*, by Zig Ziglar. I enjoyed both of these books for basically the same reason, which is that they make you understand that success cannot be obtained without overcoming problems.

The main problem we all have is winning the battle with ourselves. Consequently, I'm always looking for things that will give me an edge. I've often felt that how we react to books is basically determined by the mood we are in when we read them. If we're really down and depressed, one book may mean something to us and another one may not; and yet a week later if we read the same book, it may be just completely the opposite.

"Attitudes do make the difference. Salesman with the right attitude beat their quotas; students with the right attitude make A's; right attitudes pave the way to really happy married life. Right attitudes make you effective in dealing with people, enable you to develop as a leader. Right attitudes win for you in every situation.

"Grow these three attitudes. Make them your allies in everything you do.

1. Grow the attitude of *I'm activated*.
2. Grow the attitude of *You are important*.
3. Grow the attitude of *Service first*."

In Search of Excellence

by Thomas Peters and Robert Waterman
Recommended by: Tom Hopkins,
Author, Sales Trainer

In Search of Excellence. In today's business world, it is evident that all industries are being affected by the tremendous changes that are taking place in our society.

Over the last 20 years, concepts of management and techniques of employee motivation have changed drastically. This book gives philosophy, theory and proven strategies of some of the finest run companies in our country. Many companies want to increase their employees' effectiveness and skills, but the true need is in management training. For this reason, this book is not only timely but certainly is in tune with the needs of our times.

If you look back at the companies that went bankrupt from 1980 through 1982, there are many lessons to be learned. This book pinpoints the reasons why some companies prospered during the recessionary times and some did not. If you study the products and marketing techniques of growing companies, you can learn why many business colleges are turning out management leaders who are not sensitive to the needs and desires of employees at all levels of an organization.

In Search of Excellence is a must for anyone interested in streamlining a company for increased net profit during the next decade.

Lee Iacocca and Books

(Excerpts from his Autobiography)

"Most of all, as I lay flat on my back, I turned to books. I read like crazy—everything I could get my hands on. . . .

"I must have read my share of schoolbooks, too, because each year in high school I graduated near the top of my class, with straight A's in math. . . .

"By the time I was ready for college, I had a solid background in the fundamentals: reading, writing, and public speaking. With good teachers and the ability to concentrate, you can go pretty far with these skills.

"Years later, when my kids asked me what courses to take, my advice was always to get a good liberal arts education. Although I'm a great believer in the importance of learning from history, I really didn't care if they mastered all the dates and places of the Civil War. The key is to get a solid grounding in reading and writing."

Dropping Your Guard

by Charles Swindoll
Recommended by: Col. James B. Irwin,
President, High Flight Foundation,
Astronaut, Author, Lecturer

"Our technological age has made us more aware of
our smallness." The voyage to the moon gave me a new
perspective of the earth. I thought – if the earth is only
that small, like a marble, how small am I? I am just a
speck in the universe. Really much less than a speck,
but we all are just specks. God loves us little specks
so much. He has given each one of us the desire,
capacity and way to know Him in a personal way. In
knowing God, we are more than specks, more than
earthlings.

There is a tendency to build up walls or barriers in
our relationships with others and with God. Chuck
Swindoll's book, *Dropping Your Guard*, will give you new
insight into the value of open relationships. We learn
that there is hope if we will just take off these phony
masks. Since my return to earth I have tried to be completely open and truthful in my relationships but occasionally I need to be reminded. Chuck did an excellent
job of reminding me of my human nature and challeng-
ing me to be "accountable."

The God You Can Know

by Dan DeHaan
Recommended by: Al Jackson,
NFL, Atlanta Falcons

This book gives you a real insight on how you can get to know the Lord. It also describes methods you can take to get closer to God.

"God's glory is the total manifestation of all His attributes. His glory is what will make heaven what it will be. There will be no hindrance to God's brightness and no shadow cast upon God's glory because of sin. People have asked me how eternal life can last forever. We have the answer to that question when we understand God's glory, which is so unsearchable that it will take all eternity to begin to discover. On earth we know of certain attributes of God, but they constitute only a small part of God's nature. Their function is to relate God's character to us while we are here on earth. Imagine what He is saving for us to discover throughout all eternity. Understanding His glory will become a never-ending adventure.

"Nowhere in the Bible does God try to prove His existence. But, have you ever considered how much more difficult it is to disprove God's existence? Napoleon, while standing one night on the deck of a ship, was asked, 'Is there a God?' On hearing the question, he raised his hand and, pointing to the starry firmament, simply responded 'Gentlemen, who made all that?'

"What God longs to teach us is that when we have nothing left but God, God is enough. We find ourselves chasing so many different things. But when God's glory is known and truly desired, we will settle for nothing less. At Christ's birth the angels said, 'Glory to God in the highest.' That will be the motto of heaven for all eternity."

Triumph Born of Tragedy

by Andre Thornton and Al Jansson
Recommended by: Terry Jackson,
NFL, Seattle Seahawks

This book shows the true realization that through suffering a person grows by strength in Jesus Christ and develops a willingness to thank God for everything, because He is truly a good God and is in control.

Thousands have already been encouraged by Andre Thornton's inspiring story: "It was the most unimaginable nightmare. In the mist of total darkness I was searching for those most precious to me. I struggled to maintain my footing on the icy pavement. I was enveloped in darkness and the only sound was the wind, howling as if someone had turned on a sound track to a horror movie."

Andre Thornton's nightmare turned out to be a reality. On an icy turnpike his car overturned with his wife and two children trapped inside. An hour later, he learned the awful news as if, "a limb had been cruelly amputated from my body. Where does a man go when those whom he loves dearest are suddenly without warning wrenched from his life?"

For Andre Thornton there was only one place to go. Years spent nurturing and developing a relationship with God were his sole source of strength. Could God feel such agonizing pain? Could He put the pieces of Andre's life back together? Could any good come from such a devastating tragedy?

In the following weeks and months, Andre found answers to those questions and discovered God's incredible powers to heal even the most agonizing hurt. He learned that he could indeed experience "triumph born of tragedy."

On Becoming a Person

by Carl Rogers
Recommended by: Lee H. Javitch,
Founder, Giant Foods

Almost everyone would say how difficult it is to choose the one book which most influenced them. It's like asking which one friend has had the greatest impact. Each one has, in a different way.

In looking through my library, I stopped at *On Becoming a Person,* by Carl Rogers. I remember with fondness how this book helped me many years ago in terms of developing my own personal attitudes. It was helpful to me in my personal growth, independence and creativity. The book moved me a long way toward developing a philosophy of life and changed my approach toward people.

"In my relations with persons I have found that it does not help, in the long run, to act as though I were something that I am not. It does not help to act calm and pleasant when actually I am angry and critical. It does not help to act as though I know the answers when I do not. It does not help for me to act as though I were a loving person if actually, at the moment, I am hostile. It does not help for me to act as though I were full of assurance, if actually I am frightened and unsure. Even on a very simple level, I have found that this statement seems to hold. It does not help for me to act as though I were well when I feel ill."

"Man builds no structure which outlives a book."
—E. F. Ware

Thomas Jefferson and Aristotle

Dr. Raymond Muncy,
Professor of History, Harding University

Thomas Jefferson, who regarded his role in founding the University of Virginia a greater contribution to mankind than his service as President of the United States, was a student of Aristotle. The most important artifacts at Monticello are not his inventions, such as the dumbwaiter and the indoor weather indicator, but the books from which he gleaned his ideas. His copy of Aristotle's *Nicomachean Ethics* is well worn from many hours of study. Ideas have consequences. Jefferson realized the motivating power of ideas. During the course of debate with four others who served on the committee to draw up the Declaration of Independence, he struck out the third part of John Locke's trilogy of "life, liberty, and property," as the inalienable rights of man and replaced it with Aristotle's "pursuit of happiness." To my knowledge, this is the only document that asserts man's inalienable rights to "life, liberty, and the pursuit of happiness." It was Jefferson, the educator, the thinker, the philosopher, who struggled to give this nation direction in its infancy.

"An investment in knowledge always pays the best interest."

—Benjamin Franklin

Move Ahead With Possibility Thinking
by Dr. Robert Schuller
Recommended by: Nick Jent,
Vice-President, National Sales, U.S. Telephone

I would recommend the book *Move Ahead With Possibility Thinking*.

Dr. Schuller's personal experience has proven that dreams are possible and goals can be achieved. He breaks goals into realistic increments that make them achievable. He emphasizes that accomplishing goals necessitates taking risks: risks of embarrassment, failure, ridicule and doubt. However, you must act on your beliefs, regardless of the criticism from many of the "impossible" thinkers. Dr. Schuller also emphasizes what I call the "now" concept. Act Now! Even though you do not have all the facts and all the answers, get started. Act on your beliefs. One of the many quotes that I feel emphasizes this fact is, "I would rather attempt to do something great and fail, than attempt to do nothing and succeed." I firmly believe you have to act, and believe in what you are acting on.

Accomplishing goals also requires using resources and using them wisely. Resources such as people and ideas are precious and should not be wasted. They are resources that, when functioning in an organized manner, are keys to success. Life's goals are established to be accomplished, and as Dr. Schuller states many times, "Have faith as a grain of mustard seed and you can tell the mountain to move and nothing is impossible." I believe this book puts realism and possibility into the goals of every human being.

The Pursuit of God

by A. W. Tozer
Recommended by: Paul Johnson,
President, Paul H. Johnson Incorporated

One of my favorite authors is A. W. Tozer. Although everything he's written is great, one of his finest books, in my opinion, is *The Pursuit of God*. I try to read it at least once a year. It's only 128 pages in paperback and it helps me to see the big picture and to keep all things concerning my relationship with God in the proper perspective. It gives a clear cut plan and tells what is often painfully necessary for a full and meaningful relationship with God.

I think Chapter Two is a classic. It is entitled, "The Blessedness of Possessing Nothing." Tozer describes how "things" can so easily take the place of God in our lives. He uses the example of Abraham and Isaac in Genesis 22 to illustrate how Isaac, Abraham's prized possession, had begun to come between him and God. The relationship, as Tozer puts it, "bordered upon the perilous" and had to be dealt with.

As a Building Contractor and Real Estate Developer, I deal with real property and the acquisition of valuable things every day. I constantly need to be aware that all that I have belongs to God. Although we may "own" a lot of things, we are most blessed when we have a close and primary relationship with God and an attitude of actually possessing nothing.

The book is refreshing and heart-searching. Step by step, it shows us how to enjoy the deep things of God and how to enjoy His glory in our daily lives.

Think and Grow Rich

by Napoleon Hill
Recommended by: Mary Kay Ash,
CEO, Mary Kay Cosmetics

Napoleon Hill's *Think and Grow Rich* once turned my life around when I was at a very low point:

"Every person who wins in any undertaking must be willing to burn his ships and cut all sources of retreat. Only by doing so can one be sure of maintaining that state of mind known as a burning desire to win, essential to success.

"Opportunity has spread its wares before you. Step up to the front, select what you want, create your plan, put the plan into action, and follow through with persistence. 'Capitalistic' America will do the rest. You can depend upon this much – capitalistic America insures every person the opportunity to render useful service, and to collect riches in proportion to the value of the service.

"When you begin to think and grow rich, you will observe that riches begin with a state of mind, with definiteness of purpose, with little or no hard work. You, and every other person, ought to be interested in knowing how to acquire that state of mind which will attract riches. I spent twenty-five years in research because I, too, wanted to know 'how wealthy men become that way.'

"Before success comes in any man's life, he is sure to meet with much temporary defeat, and, perhaps, some failure. When defeat overtakes a man, the easiest and most logical thing to do is to quit. That is exactly what the majority of men do."

The Imitation of Christ

by Thomas a Kempis
Recommended by: William H. Keeler,
Bishop of Harrisburg, Pennsylvania

During student days, I recall hearing read aloud and then reading for myself an extraordinary book.

Its chapters were not long, each unfolding a theme in clear, uncluttered sentences. These sentences impressed themselves on my memory and through the years have nourished both attitudes and prayer.

There is some mystery about the monk who was the author, about his name, his place and date of birth. He is customarily identified as the German-born Thomas a Kempis, who edited the work and who died in the Netherlands in 1471, at the age of 91.

His extraordinary book, *The Imitation of Christ*, reveals a person who read, prayed over, absorbed and digested the Bible, especially the New Testament. He tried personally to walk, in his own day, as he thought Jesus had called him to walk. His dialogues of student and Master made the Lord's words come alive for me, as for many another. To ponder the pages of this book today, even briefly, is to step into the company of a faithful disciple who knows how to share inspiration and dedication.

The opening sentences give the flavor of the work: "'He that follows me shall not walk in darkness, says the Lord' (John 8:12). These are the words of Christ by which we are urged to imitate his life and virtues, if we wish to be truly enlightened and freed from all blindness of heart. Therefore, let it be our chief business to meditate upon the life of Jesus Christ."

Great Thoughts About Books

Except a living man there is nothing more wonderful than a book! – a message to us from the dead – from human souls we never saw, and who lived perhaps thousands of miles away; and yet these words on those little sheets of paper speak to us, amuse us, and comfort us.

– Kingsley

If a book is worth reading, it is worth buying.

– John Ruskin

When I get a little money, I buy books; and if any is left, I buy food and clothes.

– Erasmus

The foolishest book is a kind of leaky boat on a sea of wisdom; some of the wisdom will get in anyhow.

– Oliver Wendell Holmes

I love to lose myself in other men's minds.
When I am not walking, I am reading;
I cannot sit and think. Books think for me.

– Charles Lamb

The Thoughts of
Marcus Aurelius Antoninus

Translated by John Jackson
Recommended by: Russell Kirk,
Author, Columnist

Throughout my life, I have been comforted by the meditations of the great emperor-philosopher Marcus Aurelius, a conscience speaking to a conscience; it is as if one were conversing with a dear friend. Here is a representative passage:

"In the morning, when thou risest sore against thy will, summon up this thought: 'I am rising to do the work of a man. Why then this peevishness, if the way lies open to perform the tasks which I exist to perform, and for whose sake I was brought into the world? Or am I to say I was created for the purpose of lying in the blankets and keeping myself warm?'—'At all events, that is a more pleasant theory.'—'So the goal of thy existence is pleasure and, generally, passivity rather than activity? Look at the tiny plants and birds, at the ants, spiders, and bees: they are all doing their own work, all striving to set their little corner of the universe in order. And thou seest this, and wilt not take up thy man's burden and run the race that Nature bids thee!'—'But we must have some rest.'—Agreed: but Nature has prescribed limits to that rest, exactly as she has to eating and drinking. Yet these thou art eager enough to overstep; but come to action, and there is no thought of breaking the bounds of the possible!"

Every man is a volume if you know how to read him.
—Channing

Federalist Papers
by Hamilton, Madison and Jay
Recommended by Jeane J. Kirkpatrick,
Former Ambassador United Nations
(From Dictatorships and Double Standards)

The FOUNDING FATHERS' ROOTS in English history and their identification with the rights of Englishmen – rights won by specific persons at specific times and places – doubtless helped them to avoid the utopian expectations to which revolutionary movements are notoriously susceptible and to which the other great eighteenth-century revolution succumbed. The leaders of the American Revolution did not rely on abstract theories of historical development to guide them in what the future would be. Neither did they embrace romantic notions of "natural man" or "natural society." They did not expect that the United States would be exempt from the problems that had beset other nations. Instead of relying on American "exceptionalism," a doctrine whose force has probably been overemphasized, the framers of the American Constitution emphasized the relevance of history and of their own past experience to the former colonies' problems.

Nowhere are these modest expectations more clearly expressed than in the Constitution and in those remarkable essays written by three of the Constitution's most brilliant authors. Of these *Federalist Papers*, which remain the best source on the intentions of the Founding Fathers, Carl Van Doren asserted:

To read and understand them was the next thing to having had a hand in making the Constitution. They were widely reprinted. Their immediate influence is hard to trace, for they were without the passion and prejudice which rouse quick responses. But there can be no doubt that these papers, so rigorously anonymous at the time, made their way through the most reflective minds of the time and then on into posterity.

The Myth of the Greener Grass

by J. Allan Petersen
Recommended by: Bob Kraning, Exec. Dir.,
Forest Home Christian Conference Center

"Most of us come to marriage believing it is a box full of goodies from which we extract all we need to make us happy. The marriage license is the key to this box. We can take from it as much as we want and it somehow mysteriously remains full.

"Marriage is an empty box. There is nothing in it. It is an opportunity to put something in to do something for marriage. Marriage was never intended to do anything for anybody. People are expected to do something for marriage. If you do not put into the box more than you take out, it becomes empty. Love, romance, consideration, generosity aren't in marriage, they are in people, and people put them into the marriage box. When the box gets empty we become vulnerable to an affair.

"'One thing remains unchanged through the centuries: nothing is finer, more fulfilling—indeed, more sanctified—than the inviolate marriage bed, particularly when the decision that it will remain inviolate is the conscious act of the two people who share it.

"'There is a vast difference between wanting something when we do not have it and continuing to want it when we do have it. Continuing to desire and cherish what we have means that we have established a relationship, that we have formed an attachment—that we do, in fact, love.

"More than a century ago, Henry David Thoreau said it succinctly. 'Simplify, simplify, simplify.' Focus on, and stay true to, what is at the center, and like planets around the sun of our marriage, the other elements of life will find their right places. Be faithful, stay faithful, have faith—and happiness will happen."

Loving God

by Chuck Colson
Recommended by: Paul Kuck, President
Regal Marine Industries, Inc.

The ultimate in personal expression is *Loving God*, a magnanimous response to our Creator. When we come to the realization that what we think of as "loving God" may be, in reality, shallow or even deceptive, then we can bare our souls, clear our minds and begin to receive Colson's treatise.

Through a series of real-life narrations (experienced both personally and by others), Colson propels you from the uncomplicated "Sunday-morning-thoroughfare-of-life" into the deep recesses of the real world, where people live every day. Colson leads you through this maze and slowly but surely you experience the feeling of Light . . . and, just as surely as you see it, you meet Him who created us. This Light, what Colson calls *"Loving God"* becomes brilliantly visible in poignant narrations of God at work in the lives of people: in a prison in Delaware, in Dr. Bernie Kornfeld and Alexander Solzhenitsyn in a Russian gulag, when Colson himself is the criminal in Watergate, in the racketeer Mickey Cohen, in a judge and defendant in Indiana, in Mother Teresa in India and many other real-life events. Through it all, we are inenexorably led to the revelation that the best (perhaps the only) way to love God is to consciously obey Him, from the very depths of our being, to the best of our ability . . . And therein we must stand!!!

It is from books that wise men derive consolation in the troubles of life.

–Victor Hugo

How Should We Then Live?

by Francis A. Schaeffer
Recommended by: Tom Landry,
Coach, Dallas Cowboys

Francis Schaeffer presented two ideas that were very significant. The first is that history shows there is a swing from spiritualism to humanism that repeats itself over and over. And the second is that Christians live by absolutes. Only by this process can a person determine the changes that are taking place throughout history.

"Most people catch their presuppositions from their family and surrounding society the way a child catches measles. But people with more understanding realize that their presuppositions should be chosen after a careful consideration of what world view is true. When all is done, when all the alternatives have been explored, 'not many men are in the room'—that is, although world views have many variations there are not many basic world views or basic presuppositions. These basic options will become obvious as we look at the flow of the past.

"Rome did not fall because of external forces such as the invasion by the barbarians. Rome had no sufficient inward base; the barbarians only completed the breakdown—and Rome gradually became a ruin."

Chief Executive Officers

Passages

by Gail Sheehy
Recommended by: Ronald H. Smith,
CEO, CCNB Bank, N.A.

Of the books that I have profited from in my lifetime, one that comes to mind immediately is *Passages*. I believe that reading this book has helped me to understand the various life cycles that I have been through and those, hopefully, I will experience. It helped me to understand myself as well as customers and employees with whom I have dealings.

The March of Folly

by Barbara W. Tuchman
Recommended by: W. Paul Tippett,
CEO, American Motors Corporation

I recently read *The March of Folly*, by Barbara Tuchman, and was impressed by the painstaking research done by the author, who is a distinguished American historian. Ms. Tuchman begins with the Trojan War and continues through the centuries to the Vietnam War, anatomizing America's thirty-five year involvement. It is a book that points out the fundamental causes of governmental folly. I enjoyed what Ms. Tuchman had to say because all of us should understand and demand the kind of government to which we could securely entrust our fates.

Great Thoughts About Books

The books that charmed us in youth recall the delight ever afterwards; we are hardly persuaded there are any like them, any deserving equally our affections. Fortunate if the best fall in our way during this susceptible and forming period of our lives.

—A. Bronson Alcott

Friends, books, a cheerful heart, and conscience clear
Are the most choice companions we have here.

—William Mather

In books lies the soul of the whole Past Time; the articulate audible voice of the Past, when the body and material substance of it has altogether vanished like a dream.

—Thomas Carlyle

No matter what his rank or position may be, the lover of books is the richest and the happiest of the children of men.

—John Alfred Langford

He hath never fed of the dainties that are bred of a book; he hath not eat paper, as it were; he hath not drunk ink: his intellect is not replenished; he is only an animal, only sensible in the duller parts.

—William Shakespeare

Governors

Getting Older and Staying Young

by Dr. D. D. Stonecypher
Recommended by: George M. Leader,
Leader Nursing and Rehabilitation Centers,
former Governor of Pennsylvania

There are so many misconceptions about growing old, and about the elderly in general, that I have chosen *Getting Older and Staying Young,* by Dr. D. D. Stonecypher.

He deals with the problem in such an enlightening manner that he is an inspiration to me, even after having worked with the elderly for twenty-two years, not including the years that I was Governor and established Pennsylvania's first Commissioner on the Aging.

What we do with our lives, physically, spiritually and mentally when we are young pretty much determines what we will be in "all departments" when we are old. What resources we have available when we are old is also dependent on how well we continue to stimulate the various segments of our lives. There ought to be big warning signs along the highways of life that say in red letters, "stagnation kills;" or conversely, "stimulation keeps you alive."

Dr. Stonecypher says it much better in his book. He calls it The Law of Aging. "This law states, those functions (physical or mental) which are exercised, tend to persist, those which are not exercised, tend to disappear."

Those who obey this law may very well join thousands of others in their 80's, 90's, and 100's who are keen-witted and vigorous and creative.

Governors

Missal Romanis

Recommended by: Mario Cuomo,
Governor, New York

The book that has had the greatest effect on my life is no longer readily available. It's the *Missal Romanis,* comprising the prayers and scriptural texts of the daily liturgy of the Roman Catholic Church before the reforms instituted by the Second Vatican Council in the sixties.

In the Baltimore Catechism, Catholics of my generation learned the rules of and the rationale behind the religion they practiced. The beautiful words of the *Missal Romanis,* translated from the Latin, added emotion to the pragmatism. They enabled us to "feel" the strength of church tradition and to live at times exaltedly within that tradition.

War and Peace

by Leo Tolstoy
Recommended by: Thomas Kean,
Governor, New Jersey

Of all the books I've read, I would have to say that there is no greater one than *War and Peace,* a brilliant work by a fascinating man.

Profiles in Courage

by John F. Kennedy
Recommended by: Richard Lamm,
Governor, Colorado

Governors

The Marvelous Career of Theodore Roosevelt

by Charles Morris
Recommended by: James R. Thompson,
Governor, Illinois

I am a great fan and admirer of Theodore Roosevelt and have read numerous books on T.R.'s life. A particular favorite was *The Marvelous Career of Theodore Roosevelt*, by Charles Morris.

The Silver Chalice

by Thomas Costain
Recommended by: Martha Collins,
Governor, Kentucky

The Silver Chalice, by Thomas Costain, has always been a favorite of mine and has meant a great deal to me.

Constitution of the State of Hawaii

Recommended by: George Ariyoshi,
Governor, Hawaii

As an attorney, legislator, and Governor, my life has been most influenced by the *Constitution of the State of Hawaii*, the *Hawaii Revised Statutes*, and the *Hawaii State Plan*. These volumes contain much of the philosophy of Hawaii's people and are the basis for Hawaii's success as the 50th State of the Union.

Living Positively One Day at a Time

by Dr. Robert Schuller
Recommended by: Joe Larson, CPAE,
President, Sparta Brush Company

My book suggestion is *Living Positively One Day at a Time*, by Dr. Robert Schuller. He has written so many now, but this one helped me at a time that was very difficult. Three years ago my wife passed away, my son had a heart attack and the factory burned down – all within six months. Schuller's chapter on "Turn Your Scars Into Stars" was a great help in our response. It helped me believe that it is not what happens to you that is important . . . it is how you respond that really matters:

"As you pray up your problems – no matter how big or small, you'll find yourself becoming more and more in tune with God. Through Jesus Christ we have a direct line to God. He'll hear your prayers. They'll get through, and God's promises to those who know Him are overflowing. Look back at the lives of those you studied yesterday. They all received God's presence and peace through their pain. David, Paul, Job, Mary and Stephen were all heirs to God's promises. All they had to do was pray! Today we have the privilege to pray through Christ. He is our connection to God.

"I've done a lot of talking with Jesus and I know he listens. I know he's turning my scars into stars! If anybody is near me when I come to the point in my life when I draw my feet into bed for the last time, I will say to that person only one thing, 'When I die, play it down and pray it up! Because I know where I'm going and who will be there. His name is Jesus Christ.'"

Lawrence of Arabia and Books

Lawrence began in early childhood to lead expeditions, to study soldiery and to read of warfare. At nine and a half he was making his first brass rubbings of knights in armor, and at fifteen he was reading treatises on techniques of warfare and military castle building.

During the years in which he was an Oxford undergraduate, he prepared himself further for the major acts and events of his life. He traveled in France, and studied its castles and military architecture. He became imbued with the military, psychological and philosophical themes of the Crusades, and above all with the romantic literature of medieval France.

This literature supplied the Crusaders with an ideology that could ennoble, if not the deeds themselves, at least what motivated them, and could help to rationalize the excesses of their behavior. These works were the principal literary sustenance of Lawrence's youth. . . .

Although Lawrence read widely, his reading was dominated by medieval romantic works, especially French, and the ideas of medieval romanticism came to fill his consciousness.

—John E. Mack

Histories do rather set forth the pomp of business than the true and inward resorts thereof. But Lives, if they be well written, propounding to themselves a person to represent, in whom actions both greater and smaller, public and private, have a commixture, must of necessity contain a more true, native, and lively representation.

—Lord Bacon

Olympic Gold Medalists

Poems That Touch the Heart

Compiled by A. L. Alexander
Recommended by: Sammy Lee, M.D.

The book I always refer to whenever there is a marriage, or a tragedy, a broken romance, or death, is *Poems That Touch the Heart*, compiled by A. L. Alexander and published by Doubleday.

I often send a letter to grieving parents or a spouse and include the inspiring story of the "Dark Candle," which so poignantly tells us that all the tears, remorse, and grief will not bring her or him back to us. It tells me that our loss should be taken in stride and rejoice that the life hereafter earned by the departed one should not be dampened by our sadness. My other favorite is "Should You Go First." When you read it you will understand why I like it, and often read it. There are other poems and anecdotes which the reader will fit any of our human emotions.

How to Develop Self-Confidence and Influence People by Public Speaking

by Dale Carnegie
Recommended by: Bob Richards, CPAE

This is the book that helped me most as a professional speaker.

Barnard Baruch: The Adventures of a Wall Street Legend

by James Grant
Recommended by: Lew Lehrman,
Chairman, Citizens for America
Founder of Rite Aid

"Dorothy Parker once said two things confused her: the theory of the zipper and the exact function of Bernard Baruch. If by function Mrs. Parker meant a salaried, everyday job, Baruch was without one for most of his adult life. As a self-made millionaire he did not need one, and as a man who, in the public arena, would rather advise than act, he usually did not want one. In 1903, at the age of thirty-three, he gave up a lucrative partnership in a Wall Street brokerage firm in order to invest and speculate with his own money. In this he succeeded brilliantly, though not without suffering an occasional loss that (as he put it) 'would make an ordinary married man go out and shoot himself.'"

So begins James Grant's compelling biography of Bernard Baruch – the story of the energy, intellect, and gambler's nerve that propelled him to distinguished careers on Wall Street and in public service. BERNARD BARUCH: THE ADVENTURES OF A WALL STREET LEGEND is a riveting portrait of a man who "preferred sunshine to any office" and, given the chance, chose to work behind the scenes as an advisor to Presidents, confidante of politicians, and through the press, a public policy spokesman to the country at large. The richness of this work lies in its illustration of the vain and virtuous Baruch, the financial operator as well as the complex public figure. Here is the history of a life of great activity that could be the stuff of several successful careers.

Incentive Management

by James F. Lincoln
Recommended by: Dr. Richard Le Tourneau,
President, Le Tourneau College

A book that has influenced my approach to motivation and management, *Incentive Management*, was by the founder of Lincoln Electric, J. F. Lincoln. The book tells how they were able to get their employees to produce a superior product which would sell at half the price. At the same time, employees were paid twice the going wage.

"We see here the reason why socialism, communism, the welfare state or any kind of government that gives security to the individual must fail. It also shows why the economy that does not pose problems to the individual that he cannot easily solve will be taken over by the economy that does. Individual responsibility is essential to strength. The individual who throws his responsibility for himself on the state will become soft, static and unprogressive.

"Socialism or any other form of welfare state must fail, since it cannot develop citizens who will make a successful economy. This is not obvious at first to those who want to believe that responsibility can be shifted to someone else or by the coward who does not want to deal with reality in life. He can always make a good case for his idea that the state should make him secure because he is a citizen.

"It is obvious that such possible progress under incentive management would pose new problems to the economy. There is little doubt, however, that economic progress so far has resulted in a more attractive human race, as well as a more attractive living. The new problems posed by this progress will be solved by men who are developed as incentive management will develop them. Man will gain in stature as a consequence."

Creation in Christ:
Unspoken Sermons

by George MacDonald
Recommended by: C. S. Lewis 1898–1963
(From God in the Dock)

George MacDonald I had found for myself at the age of sixteen and never wavered in my allegiance though I tried for a long time to ignore his Christianity.

The Use Of Fear

"Naturally the first emotion of man towards the being he calls God, but of whom he knows so little, is fear.

"Where it is possible that fear should exist, it is well it should exist, cause continual uneasiness, and be cast out by nothing less than love. In him who does not know God, and must be anything but satisfied with himself, fear towards God is as reasonable as it is natural, and serves powerfully towards the development of his true humanity. Neither the savage, nor the self-sufficient sage, is rightly human. It matters nothing whether we regard the one or the other as degenerate or as undeveloped — neither I say is human; the humanity is there, but has to be born in each and for this birth everything natural must do its part.

"Fear is natural, and has a part to perform nothing but itself could perform in the birth of the true humanity. Until love, which is the truth towards God, is able to cast out fear, it is well that fear should hold; it is a bond, however poor, between that which is and that which creates — a bond that must be broken, but a bond that can be broken only by the tightening of an infinitely closer bond."

Lincoln & Poetry

Those long-lived and erstwhile companions who, in later years, trafficked in remembering Lincoln were agreed that he had an inexhaustible, if sometimes curious, appreciation of Poetry. Best of all they remember his admiration for Burns and Shakespeare, and frequently mated those outward imcompatibles in their commentaries.

Howells conjoined the Scot and the Englishman when he wrote in his book, "Before his (i.e., Lincoln's) election to Congress, a copy of Burns was his inseparable companion on the circuit; and this he perused so constantly, that it is said he has now by heart every line of his favorite poet. He is also a diligent student of Shakespeare, 'to know whom is a liberal education.'"

Milton Hay thought that Mr. Lincoln "could very nearly quote all of Burns' poems from memory." He had frequently heard him recite The Whole of **Tam O'Shanter, Holy Willie's Prayer** and large portions of the **Cotter's Saturday Night**. According to Hay, Mr. Lincoln had acquired the Scotch accent and could render Burns perfectly.

—David C. Mearns
Windsor Lectures, 1955

Abraham Lincoln

by Carl Sandburg
Recommended by: Art Linkletter,
CPAE, Author, TV Personality

In the biographical category, which is my favorite, I would have to put Carl Sandburg's three volumes on Abraham Lincoln: *The Prairie Years* (1809–1861), *The War Years* (1861–1864) and *The War Years* (1864–1865). In his remarkable life, Abe Lincoln demonstrated the value of faith, persistence, and common sense. He is an inspiration that shines out in American history like a beacon.

Secondly, I would leap to modern times and suggest *Future Shock*, by Alvin Toffler, which is a practical, incisive tool for helping us to survive our collision with tomorrow. He writes, "In the three short decades between now and the twenty-first century, millions of ordinary, psychologically normal people will face an abrupt collision with the future." Yet *Future Shock* is about the present. It is about what is happening today, exploring the hidden impact of change.

No list of my favorite books would be complete without the landmark Norman Vincent Peale book, *The Power of Positive Thinking*. This gentle, kind, thoughtful preacher has changed the lives of millions with his down-to-earth stories about the ways in which positive thought controls and shapes our destiny.

Finally, I would pick a small, incisive book called *The Drug Dilemma* by Sidney Cohen.

Douglas MacArthur and Books

"In September 1893, my father was ordered to Texas. I hailed this move with delight. Housing the largest garrison I had ever seen, Fort Sam Houston guarded our southern borders and was one of the most important posts in the Army. It was here that a transformation began to take place in my development. I was enrolled in the West Texas Military Academy headed by the Reverend Allen Burlesoa, rector of the Army chapel. There came a desire to know, a seeking for the reason why, a search for the truth. Abstruse mathematics began to appear as a challenge to analysis, dull Latin and Greek seemed a gateway to the moving words of the leaders of the past laborious historical data led to the nerve-tingling battlefields of the great captains. Biblical lessons began to open the spiritual portals of a growing faith, literature to lay bare the souls of men. My studies enveloped me, my marks went higher, and many of the school medals came my way. But I also learned how little such honors mean after one wins them."

An educated man stands, as it were, in the midst of a boundless arsenal and magazine, filled with all the weapons and engines which man's skill has been able to devise from the earliest time.

−Thomas Carlyle

Churchill

Taken from the Diaries of Lord Morgan
Recommended by: Richard Mahoney,
CEO, Monsanto

This is the best book I've read during a long study of Churchill I've engaged in for years. William Manchester's book is also excellent. They both describe overcoming adversity, turning liabilities into assets, and the mass movement of minds.

"For a young boy to create a fantasy father and to sustain that fantasy for many years was remarkable indeed. It showed an ability to forge the required conditions of his development. He had built the model he wanted to follow. It showed an unusual capacity to integrate illusion and reality, to tolerate different perspectives. In later years, he would pursue schemes, no matter how farfetched, with obstinate energy. He would integrate different elements of his nature, the humane and the ruthless, the dreamer and the man of action, in a way that most people cannot. Most people cannot tolerate so many different facets and the tensions they create. They are baffled and upset by inconsistency. They break down, or their behavior becomes pathological. But Churchill was able to adopt contradictory points of view with equal brilliance and insight, and an equal sense of conviction about the rightness of his position, investing it with a deeply felt moral authority. He had done it as a child, when he invented his own version of his father, and he would do it again, at every step of his political ascent."

Goodbye, Darkness

by William Manchester
Recommended by: John Majors,
Football Coach, Univ. of Tennessee

I have read many inspirational books but I will mention one in particular that I could hardly put down
while reading – *Goodbye, Darkness*, by William Manchester.

I could hardly wait to read it each evening when I
came home from work. It is a poignant book regarding
the U.S. Marines' campaign in the South Pacific in
World War II. It is one of the most realistic books I
can imagine. Many young men, great Americans and
our Allies, gave their lives, their bodies and souls, and
whatever it took, to give us the liberty that we enjoy
today. For this we should all be truly grateful.

"Screaming, 'Banzai!' they charged. Riflemen of the
First Marines picked them off while our 37-millimeter
canister shells exploded on the sandspit. The enemy's
first wave altered; then a second wave came on, and
then a third. Because the wire was inadequate – thousands of spools had left with Fletcher's ships – some
of the attackers got through. Three of them rushed the
foxhole of a corporal firing a BAR. The BAR jammed.
Shouting Marine, you die!' one Nip jumped into the
hole. The corporal grabbed his machete and cut the
Nip down; then he jumped the other two Japs and hack-
ed them, too, to death. One Marine machine gunner
was killed; his rigid finger remained locked on the trigger, scything the enemy. Blinded by a grenade, Al
Schmid, another machine gunner, continued to fire,
directed by his dying buddy."

Our Useless Fears

by Dr. John Wolpe
Recommended by: Richard M. Marcks,
President, Hershey International Ltd.

Dr. Wolpe was the founder of "systematic desensitization," which is now used widely by psychologists in helping people reduce anxieties. In contrast to psychocybernetics, which deals with mental processes and mental discipline in bringing about an intellectual and rational response to situations, Wolpe's book deals with such problems on an emotional plane by providing a "relaxation response" for meeting anxiety.

I was quite impressed with this book and have tried the step-by-step relaxation procedure proposed by Dr. Wolpe in meeting various kinds of stress and tight situations. I believe the technique is somewhat allied to the one recommended for meditation in the book, *Relaxation Response*. In the midst of a jumbled, complex, and tedious day, 15 minutes of meditation or complete relaxation can go a long way toward re-energizing your thoughts and level of physical activity. Aside from the relaxation technique I have just described, Wolpe also discloses and explains his technique of "systematic desensitization," which provides persons suffering from acute anxiety ways to "desensitize" themselves by gradually becoming familiar, in little steps or doses, with the thing that is feared.

After reading Dr. Wolpe's book, I am sure you will be able to capsulize better than I have, this notion which is used widely by clinical psychologists around the country.

Folkways

by William Sumner
Recommended by: Stanley Marcus, President,
Neiman-Marcus department store, Author

What *Folkways* did for me was sort of open new doors into new horizons of the history of humanity, of the human race. It taught me the important word which he more or less brought into common usage, the word *mores*.

It made me recognize that there are more than one or two ways of doing anything in life, and the way that the aborigine in Australia might do a commonplace thing was good for him even though we considered it bad.

Throughout my adult life, I've maintained an interest in archaeology and anthropology purely as an amateur, but now I'm married to a woman who is studying to get her Ph.D. in archaeology. So the book has made me much more understanding of her work, as well as giving me a better understanding of the world.

A reader cannot be more rationally entertained than by comparing and drawing a parallel between his own private character and that of other persons.

—Addison

The Greatest Salesman in the World

by Og Mandino
Recommended by: J. W. Marriott,
President, Marriott Hotels

I profited from Og Mandino's *Greatest Salesman in the World*, and gave a copy to each of our marketing executives.

"Henceforth, I will learn and apply another secret of those who excel in my work. When each day is ended, not regarding whether it has been a success or a failure, I will attempt to achieve one more sale. When my thoughts beckon my tired body homeward, I will resist the temptation to depart. I will try again. I will make one more attempt to close with victory, and if that fails I will make another. Never will I allow any day to end with a failure. Thus will I plant the seed of tomorrow's success and gain an insurmountable advantage over those who cease their labor at a prescribed time. When others cease their struggle, then mine will begin, and my harvest will be full.

"Nor will I allow yesterday's success to lull me into today's complacency, for this is the great foundation of failure. I will forget the happenings of the day that is gone, whether they were good or bad, and greet the new sun with confidence that this will be the best day of my life.

"So long as there is breath in me, that long will I persist. For now I know one of the greatest principles of success; if I persist long enough I will win."

Psycho-Cybernetics

by Maxwell Maltz, M.D.
Recommended by: R.C.A. Martin, Chairman,
Pa. National Mutual Casualty Insurance Co.

This book deals with self-image, or what you think of yourself. Self-image pretty well circumscribes a man's limits, his capacities, his ambitions, his desires to succeed and accomplish. Dr. Maltz, being a plastic surgeon, points to the fact that by applying the proper remedy, removing the blemishes and other physical anomalies will change a person's attitude, their personality, their self-image and, in the doing, will increase the area of one's possibilities and broaden one's capabilities. I concluded there was a psychological approach and a clinical approach to the treatment of self-image.

But I also make the observation that sometimes we do not want to change too much. We want to hang on to some old fetish, to pity ourselves. The story is told of a plastic surgeon who, upon seeing a tremendously homely man in the subway, offered to perform surgery necessary to improve his looks, at no charge. The man, fully aware of his condition, gratefully agreed. The doctor, wanting some guidance, asked the patient what size nose he wanted, the shape of his mouth, etc., and advised him that he could make him the most handsome man around, that he could change his face completely. The patient replied, "Well, now don't change me too much, I just want to make sure that all of my friends know who this handsome man is."

Something More

by Catherine Marshall
Recommended by: General Robert C. Mathis,
USAF Ret.

Some years ago, when I felt empty although I was apparently succeeding in my military career, my wife handed me Catherine Marshall's *Something More*. In reading the book, I found it opened a totally new way of life for me. I knew there would be no going back. I think the feeling is expressed well in her book on page 161:

"Whenever anyone sets up his reasoning against God's, he is going the Aquinas way of humanistic autonomy, even though he may piously call it faith. The only true wisdom is facing up to what we actually are – creatures – and then yielding ourselves to the love and wisdom of our Creator. This yielding is relinquishment. And as we relinquish our own defective, incomplete human judgment, it feels like death because it is death – the beginning of the end of the old Adam in us."

A good book is the precious life-blood of a master spirit, imbalmed and treasured up on purpose to a Life beyond Life.

–Milton, *Areopagitica*. Sec. 6

Roget's Thesaurus

by Peter Mark Roget
Recommended by: Arthur I. Melvin, Ph.D.,
Exec. Dir., Century 111 Foundation

Please don't laugh at my recommendation of this exceptional book: *Roget's Thesaurus*. Rather, convince yourself by investing an hour to review its introductory "Plan of Classification and Synopsis of Categories." You will more clearly grasp both the complexity and orderliness of everyday ideas which are further demonstration not only of the wisdom of the Creator, but also His infinite love to place within each person an orderly latent matrix of moral common sense to guide us in coping with the complexities of life.

For example, turn to the index and investigate the ideas listed in each section to determine the depth of meaning communicated by the words which make up the title for the book you are now reading:

People: kinsfolk – 11; multitude – 102; inhabit – 186; mankind – 372; commonality – 876; laity – 997.

Meet: agreement – 23; assemble – 72; touch – 199; converge – 290; arrive – 292; expedient – 646; fulfill – 772; etc.

And: addition – 37; accompaniment – 88.

Books: Publish – 531; record – 551; volume – 593; script – 599; memory – 505; of books – 985.

Read: interpretation – 522; learning – 539; knowledge – 490.

Frequent reference to *Roget's Thesaurus* increases conviction that we too often misunderstand the intended meaning in each other's words. To compensate for the potential confusion, I am convinced each person needs to take time to discover the inextricable interrelationships of reality principles which form the moral standard existing within, though often buried under cultural smog.

Celebration of Discipline

by Richard Foster
Recommended by: Ronald L. Mercer, V.P., Xerox

In his foreword to *Celebration of Discipline*, D. Elton Trueblood says, "There are many books concerned with the inner life, but there are not too many that combine real originality with intellectual integrity. Yet, it is exactly this combination which Richard Foster has been able to produce." In his book, Richard Foster looks at the classic spiritual disciplines but in a fresh new way that, for a layman, represents a new dimension in trying to live a good, decent, upright life in a world where it seems everyone else is following the path of least resistance. His treatment of meditation, prayer, fasting, study, simplicity, solitude, submission, service, confession, worship, guidance and celebration gives new and extremely valuable insights into these disciplines which bring order to the chaos we too often find when struggling with spiritual issues.

Foster points out correctly that our happiness is not dependent on getting our way and that self denial does not mean giving up our self identity. It is actually the opposite. We are happiest when we subordinate our own personal self interests on behalf of others and we find our real identity in self denial.

This book has changed my entire view of both the word "discipline" as well as its meaning. Reading it was exciting, encouraging and personally helpful.

Reading furnishes the mind only with materials of knowledge; it is thinking makes what we read ours.
—John Locke

Coaches of Championship Basketball Teams

Profiles in Courage

by John F. Kennedy
Recommended by: Ray Meyer,
Coach, DePaul University

My selection is John F. Kennedy's *Profiles in Courage*. There are stories about four or five senators who overcame obstacles in achieving legislation. These were people who overcame physical handicaps along with mental handicaps. They had goals of justice, righteousness and harmony. These were the goals of Plato and Socrates. These senators worked not for personal gain, but for the good of mankind.

Grant and Lee

by Maj. Gen. J. F. C. Fuller
Recommended by: Bobby Knight,
Coach, Indiana University & U.S. Olympic Team

Tough Times Never Last But Tough People Do

by Dr. Robert Schuller
Recommended by: Jim Valvano,
Coach, North Carolina State

Coaches of Championship Basketball Teams

The Little Prince

by Antoine de Saint Exupery
Recommended by: Al McGuire,
Former Basketball Coach, Marquette University

The Little Prince, by Antoine de Saint Exupery, has long been a favorite of mine and is a book I've often given to friends. It illustrates the simple qualities of imagination, friendship, trust, love and loyalty that are, inevitably, the most important. It also reminds us not to lose the wonder and innocence of the little child in us. Best of all, it can be read and understood by any child from 5 to 55.

Magnificent Obsession

by Lloyd Douglass
Recommended by: John Wooden,
Former UCLA Basketball Coach, Author

The Bible, of course, is the greatest of all, but *Magnificent Obsession*, by Lloyd Douglass, made a deep impression on me; as did his, *The Robe*. I also enjoy Shakespeare, Whitman, Bryant, Tennyson, Wordsworth, Byron and many other poets.

Thomas Merton & Books

My geography book was the favorite book of my childhood. I was so fond of playing prisoner's base all over those maps that I wanted to become a sailor. I was only too eager for the kind of foot-loose and unstable life I was soon to get into.

My second best book confirmed me in this desire. This was a collection of stories called the *Greek Heroes*. It was more than I could do to read the Victorian version of these Greek myths for myself, but Father read them aloud, and I learned of Theseus and the Minotaur, of the Medusa, of Perseus and Andromeda. Jason sailed to a far land, after the Golden Fleece. Theseus returned victorious, but forgot to change the black sails, and the King of Athens threw himself down from the rock, believing that his son was dead. In those days I learned the name Hesperides, and it was from these things that I unconsciously built up the vague fragments of a religion and of a philosophy, which remained hidden and implicit in my acts, and which, in due time, were to assert themselves in a deep and all-embracing attachment to my own judgement and my own will and a constant turning away from subjection, towards the freedom of my own ever-changing horizons.

I love to lose myself in other men's minds. When I am not walking, I am reading; I cannot sit and think. Books think for me.
> —Charles Lamb, *Last Essays of Elia:*
> *Detached Thoughts on Books and Reading*

Passages

by Gail Sheehy
Recommended by: Rudolph Michaud,
Sr. V.P., Metropolitan Life Insurance Co.

Passages confirms what we already suspected – that life is a series of stages, most of which are categorically shared by everyone.

The message to be derived is that we can assist one another through life, once we understand and anticipate the predictable stages which we all share in common as adults. *Passages* helps one to understand that life can be easier to understand backwards, yet it leads one to the reality that it needs to be lived forward.

Unfortunately, prior to reading this book, I found advice on adult years in given segments was generally missing or described in abstract terms that made practical application difficult, if not impossible.

Passages has enabled me to avoid needless anxiety in my own life and has provided me with insight essential to my dealing with countless others. With this foresight, I am able to direct life's stages into very constructive and structured growth experiences.

Passages bridged many gaps for me. It reaffirmed my outlook on life. I now understand that it is an exciting and exhilarating journey which you can maximize by understanding certain predictable passages in yourself, those you know, and those you love.

Malcolm Muggeridge and Books

Excerpts from his Diaries

January 1, 1937
Kitty and I read the Book of Job aloud this evening.
I love it. I cannot see anything substantial that has
been learned about life since it was written.

January 3, 1937
Today I read, in James's *Varieties of Religious Experi-
ence*, experience after experience, particularly from
Geothe, Tolstoy, Bunyan and Luther.

November 4-7, 1949
Read Peter Quennell's *John Ruskin: The Portrait of a
Prophet* with great interest. Ruskin I find more and
more fascinating, and he would certainly be my English
"Green Stick" figure along with Tolstoy, Walt Whitman,
etc. All the contradictions of the Victorian Age and of
the Welfare State become implicit in him. His friendship with Carlyle most interesting. Consider him now
the exact equivalent of Tolstoy. His Guild of St. George,
road making, etc., all intimations of a future Welfare
State. He himself said he was "another Rousseau".
Much taken with his phrase "Nebuchadnezzar's bitter
grass".

February 17, 1962
Reading Pascal after Balzac (which I did) is like
breathing mountain air after an evening in a night
club. That lucidity! Oh, if I could capture it. Pascal died
at 39. He was in pain almost every day of his life. Yet
his life was triumphant, one of the most triumphant
ever lived.

Life of Johnson

by James Boswell
Recommended by: William Murchison,
Associate Editor, Dallas Morning News

I recommend Boswell's *Life of Johnson* for a variety
of reasons. First, for exposure to the greatest biography
ever written. Second, for exposure to the most admir-
able mind of the 18th century, Dr. Samuel Johnson. To
be sure, he was much more than Mind alone. He was
Character and Integrity personified. Third, for the
aperture created by Boswell to Johnson's own books,
which—even if written in a style unfamiliar to those
of us in the late 20th century—are full of common
sense and inspiration:

"If obedience to the will of God be necessary to happiness, and knowledge of his will be necessary to
obedience, I know not how he that withholds this
knowledge, or delays it, can be said to love his neigh-
bour as himself. He that voluntarily continues ignorance, is guilty of all the crimes which ignorance produces; as to him that should extinguish the tapers of
a light-house, might justly be imputed the calamities
of shipwrecks. Christianity is the highest perfection of
humanity; and as no man is good but as he wishes the
good of others, no man can be good in the highest
degree, who wishes not to others, the largest measures
of the greatest good."

Will Rogers, The Man And His Times

by Richard M. Ketchum
Recommended by: Bob Murphey, CPAE,
Attorney, Nacogdoches, Texas

This book details the life of Will Rogers, who has been described as America's pre-eminent humorist. He was the down-to-earth, horse-sense conscience of the nation.

A reading of this book not only gives insight into the man, Will Rogers, the most beloved figure of his time, but also presents a graphic picture of the people, events, and history of the United States during the turbulent first third of this century.

This book makes easy reading and contains many, many of Roger's quotes, comments, and quips.

A reader will close this book with a better sense of humor, a more relaxed philosophy, humility, a greater love of his country, and a respect for the simple and basic virtues of life!

"A man only learns by two things. One is reading and the other is association with smarter people."

"I just started in wrong. All educated people started in reading good books. Well, I didn't. I seem to have gone from Frank Merriwell and Nick Carter right to the Congressional Record . . . just one set of low fiction to another!"

Plain Speaking,
An Oral Biography of Harry S. Truman

by Merle Miller
Recommended by: Gordon Myers, M.D., Surgeon

Plain Speaking has been a very inspiring book to me. To quote Harry Truman, "I don't think knowing what's the right thing to do ever gives anybody too much trouble. It's doing the right thing that seems to give a lot of people trouble."

This book epitomizes what an enduring leader should be. The gist is to be loyal and supportive to your family, friends, and country.

Anyone who dares to follow the substance of this book would only move in the direction of honorable productivity. As the author states in the foreword, *Plain Speaking* is "so alive it will seem warm to the touch."

"At this moment I have in my heart a prayer. As I have assumed my heavy duties, I humbly pray to Almighty God in the words of King Solomon, 'Give therefore Thy servant an understanding heart to judge Thy people that I may discern between good and bad; for who is able to judge this Thy so great a people?' I ask only to be a good and faithful servant of my Lord and my people."

> —Harry S. Truman, from his first address to Congress after assuming the Presidency

Surprised by Joy

by C. S. Lewis
Recommended by: E. William Nash, President,
South-Central Operations, The Prudential
Insurance Company of America

At Wheaton College, I encountered Dr. Clyde S. Kilby, who introduced me to great literature and C. S. Lewis, the great English medieval scholar, critic, poet and Christian apologist.

In his biography, *Surprised by Joy*, he traces his life from early childhood in Ireland to Magdalen College, Oxford. Along the way, he encountered God, whom he thought he had dealt with as a young scholar, and accepted 'Reason' as his rule for life. But there was still an emptiness . . . the search continued. This is my favorite passage from the book:

"I perceived (and this was a wonder of wonders) that just as I have been wrong in supposing that I really desired the Garden of the Hesperides, so also I had been equally wrong in supposing that I desired Joy itself. Joy itself, considered simply as an event in my own mind, turned out to be of no value at all. All the value lay in that of which Joy was the desiring. And that object, quite clearly, was no state of my own mind or body at all. In a way, I had proved this by elimination. I had tried everything in my own mind and body; as it were, asking myself, 'Is it this you want? Is it this?' Last of all, I had asked if Joy itself was what I wanted; and, labelling it 'aesthetic experience', had pretended I proclaimed, 'You want — I myself am your want of — something other, outside, not you nor any state of you.' I did not yet ask, Who is the desired?"

The Great Marlborough and His Duchess

by Virginia Cowles
Recommended by: A. J. F. O'Reilly,
President, CEO, Heinz, Inc.

There are many biographies that recount the rise and, occasionally, the fall of great men and women who dominate their times. In the Duke and Duchess of Marlborough, you find a couple who rose to dizzying heights during a turbulent period, both making singular contributions to the political and social uplift of the British people. Yet, as happened with Winston Churchill in the wake of World War II, both spent the final years of their lives warding off attacks on their integrity. The book is a sober reminder of the fleetness of fame, the evanescent nature of success, and the vulnerability of all achievement to the onslaught of calumny from envious, most often lesser, people. This is the enduring value of the Cowles biography, while the inspiration of the volume is summed up in this quotation:

> His life mirrored the reflection of Rudyard Kipling – "who met with triumph and disaster and treated these two imposters just the same."

I am inclined to the view that we all share the common legacy of books, without which the richest would be poor.

The Road Less Traveled

by M. Scott Peck
Recommended by: Tom Osborne,
Head Football Coach, University of Nebraska

The book that I would recommend as having been most meaningful to me in recent years is *The Road Less Traveled*, by M. Scott Peck. I believe that the most memorable thing about the book to me was the discussion of discipline in Christian living.

"Spiritual power resides entirely within the individual and has nothing to do with the capacity to coerce others. People of great spiritual power may be wealthy and may upon occasion occupy political positions of leadership, but they are as likely to be poor and lacking in political authority.

"The experience of spiritual power is basically a joyful one. There is a joy that comes with mastery. Indeed, there is no greater satisfaction than that of being an expert, of really knowing what we are doing. Those who have grown the most spiritually are those who are the experts in living. And there is yet another joy, even greater, it is the joy of communion with God. For when we truly know what we are doing, we are participating in the omniscience of God."

Chief Executive Officers

The Fountainhead
by Ayn Rand
Recommended by: James Ferguson,
CEO, General Foods

Just and Unjust Ways
by Michael Walger
Recommended by: Robert Flanagan,
CEO, Western Union

Man's Search for Meaning
by Victor Frankl
Recommended by: Hugh Barker,
CEO, Public Service Company of Indiana

Politics: Who Gets What, When & How
by Harold Lasswell
Recommended by: Dan Moore, Board Chairman,
International Platform Association

Magic of Thinking Big

by David Schwartz, Ph.D.
Recommended by: Jim Parker, D.C., President,
Parker Chiropractic Research Foundation

The *Magic of Thinking Big* was a "Naturally-Right" book for me. It fit the way I was thinking about my profession, or at least the way I wanted to think about it.

It was over 20 years ago; it was a bit like another conversion. I worked at the office on Saturday and picked up the book at a bookstore on the way home and read it a bit before fulfilling a Saturday night dinner engagement. Upon returning, I began reading it again and was so energized by it, I finished it about 3 a.m. and then proceeded to go back through it, this time marking those special and inspiring parts that jumped out at me. I finished it around 9 a.m., went to the University Baptist Church, stopped for lunch and went home to sleep three hours. When I awoke, I was as fresh and energized as if I had slept the usual night through.

I think every human being who wants to grow must act one step bigger than he feels, must push himself just beyond his comfort zone. I believe that nature has a way of giving one that which he acts like he already has. The *Magic of Thinking Big* did just that for me. And it still is one of the most inspiring "how-to" and "ways-to" books in my library. Thinking big draws power to one; this book told me how.

"Some good book is usually responsible for the success of every really great man."

—Roy L. Smith

George S. Patton, Jr. and Books

General U.S. Army

There was a spinster aunt in the Patton home who devoted many hours reading to "Georgie." Her selection of books included the finest adventure stories ever written: the works of Sir Walter Scott — *Rob Roy*, the *Legend of Montrose, Kenilworth, The Pirate, The Talisman, The Tales of Crusaders*, and the immortal *Ivanhoe*; the books and poems of Rudyard Kipling — *Soldier's Three, Captains Courageous, Kim, The Seven Seas, The Jungle Book, The Three Musketeers, The Count of Monte Cristo*, and other books by Alexandre Dumas; the stories of early American pioneer days by James Fenimore Cooper — *The Spy, The Last of the Mohicans, The Prairie, The Pathfinder*, and *Deerslayer*. In the extensive library of his boyhood home were other books with which he became very familiar: *The Arabian Nights, The Corsican*, Ferror's *Greatness and Decline of Rome, Robinson Crusoe*, Sayers' *The Man Born to be King, Westward Ho*, and *King Arthur and the Knights of the Round Table*. Exposure to these classics developed a spirit of imagination and chivalry in young Patton that was part of his personality throughout his adult life.

Whenever his aunt was interrupted as she read to George and his sister, Nita, he became impatient. Georgie, snuggled up close to his beloved aunt, would look up into her eyes and say, "Read, damnit, Auntie, read." His Aunt Annie would act shocked and say to the boy she loved so much. "Now Georgie, you shouldn't say that."

—Farago

A book may be as great a thing as a battle.

—Benjamin Disraeli

Great Americans

Ulysses S. Grant and Books

"I could not sit in my room doing nothing. There is a fine library connected with the Academy from which cadets can get books to read in their quarters. I devoted more time to these than to the course of studies. Much of the time, I am sorry to say, was devoted to novels, but not those of a trashy sort. I read all of Bulwer's then published, Cooper's, Marryatt's, Scott's, Washington Irving's work, Lever's, and many others that I do not now remember."

–Grant's *Memoirs*

Robert E. Lee and Books

Robert had more time for independent reading during the late winter and early spring of 1828 than in any other period of his cadetship. Between January 27 and May 24, he drew fifty-two books from the library. They covered a wide field–navigation, travel, strategy, biography, and history. He indulged himself, moreover, in a reading of a French edition of Rousseau's *Confessions*.

Robert's reading did not interfere that spring with his studies or with his military duty. When the examinations were over in June, Robert had not headed Charles Mason but he was immediately below him on the roll of general merit. He was credited with 295 of a possible 300 in physics and was second in that subject. He stood No. 3 in chemistry, with 99 of the allowable 100. Drawing now yielded him 97 of a maximum 100 points. His general merit for the year was very high–491.

–Douglas Southall Freeman

The Success System That Never Fails

by W. Clement Stone
Recommended by: Norman Vincent Peale, CPAE,
Pastor, Author

As to a book that has meant much to me, it is W. Clement Stone's *The Success System That Never Fails*. This book outlines the secrets of success that really work. Dr. Stone has the ability to clarify the mental attitudes that overcome difficulty and adversity and motivate a person to be his most constructive self. It encourages readers to believe in themselves, to have confidence in their own potential. The ideas are valid, the writing style cogent, the effect persuasive. I think it is certainly one of the great motivational books of our time.

"You become what you think. My living philosophy is this:

"First, God is always a good God.

"Second, truth will always be truth, regardless of lack of understanding, disbelief, or ignorance.

"Third, man is the product of his heredity, environment, physical body, conscious and subconscious mind, experience, and particular position and direction in time and space . . . and something more, including powers known and unknown. He has the power to affect, use, control, or harmonize with all of them.

"Fourth, man was created in the image of God, and he has the God-given ability to direct his thoughts, control his emotions, and ordain his destiny.

"Fifth, Christianity is a dynamic, living, growing experience. But it must be applied to become alive.

"Sixth, I believe in prayer and the miraculous power of prayer."

William Penn The Scholar

Despite a conviction that an inordinate thirst for knowledge merely worsened man's condition, Penn read incessantly. This involves no contradiction. Penn, in his teens, was neither critic nor polemicist; he read not to question teachings but to store up information, to prove the truths already known. The Bible and the Christian fathers, he firmly believed, had already set down everything necessary for human guidance; all else was unessential. He was trying to understand what God had wrought, not how or why He had performed His miracles. Penn would not then have hesitated to swear his belief in the Thirty-nine Articles of Anglican faith.

He does not neglect to point out how toleration promotes national prosperity. No country, he submits, is "so improved in wealth, trade and power" as Holland. And does she not owe it to "her indulgence in matters of faith and worship?" Even the infidels, he thinks, can teach the Christian nations something: "Among the very Mahometans of Turkey and Persia, what variety of opinions, yet what unity and concord is there! We mean in matters of a civil importance." He then summons a cloud of witnesses to testify on the wisdom and justice of toleration – classical writers like Cato and Tacitus, church fathers like Justin Martyr and Tertullian, Reformers like Luther and Calvin. Monarchs like the kings of Poland and Bohemia, English writers like Sir Walter Raleigh and Jeremy Taylor and even Geoffrey Chaucer ("whose matter," he adds, "and not his poetry heartily affects me").

How much effect Penn's *The Great Case* may have had in preparing the way for that victory cannot be measured.

Beyond Success And Failure

by Willard and Marguerite Beecher
Recommended by: J. Allan Petersen,
Author, Director Family Concern

This book has no beginning or end. It doesn't go anywhere. But it is dynamite! Totally different from every other self-help book. No slogans or banners – no recently discovered secrets – no formulas to memorize – but all 240 pages are memorable. These are a series of random reflections on self-reliance and maturity by a husband and wife team of psychologists. This book is sparklingly written with powerful and penetrating insights on initiative, dependency, competition, and relationships.

The authors seem to have one overriding central objective – to demolish the scapegoat theory and enable all of us struggling humans to stop blaming others and external conditions for our failures. How we play these games in marriage is exposed. Our excuses are analyzed, dissected and so many of our problems are shown to be the result of the abdication of personal initiative, of making someone else responsible for our happiness and deficiencies.

Each page contains salty modern wisdom – insights that will affect every area of life and lead to decisive action. But before you read it, fasten your seat belt and prepare your mind and heart for a cobweb cleaning.

"The real purpose of books is to trap the mind into doing its own thinking."
–Christopher Morley

Vietnam POWs

The Right Stuff

by Thomas Wolfe
Recommended by: Lt. Cmdr. Charles Plumb,
USN Retired, Author, Professional Speaker

The Right Stuff, by Thomas Wolfe, is about "envelopes." He traces in stirring detail the early days of rocket test flight and the trials of our original seven U.S. Astronauts.

Thomas Wolfe shows how human beings have envelopes, too. Chuck Yeager, the unsung hero of test flight, pushed his physical strength and stamina to their limits that day he climbed into the X-1 and became the first man to break the forbidden sound barrier. In the same way, the wives of the original astronauts stretched their wits as their husbands put their lives on the line day after day.

An aircraft design engineer establishes the limits of an aircraft and, thus, draws the envelope of flight characteristics. But each of us sets our own parameters of physical, mental, emotional and spiritual operations and, thus, in the same way, author our own envelope for living. The person who clings to physical comfort and security lives within a smaller envelope than one who strikes out with reckless abandon. The measure of confidence and, frequently, the measure of success is determined by how close each of us comes to the stretching of our envelope. In all areas of life, each of us should strive to know our own capabilities and limits and yet not be afraid of them. And to learn this eternal truth about oneself and abide by that truth is the personal acquisition of The Right Stuff.

Vietnam POWs

Believed to be Alive

by John W. Thornton
Recommended by: Ralph Gaither,
Commander, U.S. Navy

I recommend a book titled, *Believed to be Alive*, by John W. Thornton, Capt., USN, a returned Korean POW. It is a story of courage, faith in God and Country, and tremendous will to live.

My Beloved My Friend

by Freda K. Routh
Recommended by: James A. Mulligan,
Captain, USN Retired

I have read a wonderful book called *My Beloved My Friend*. The book is only 46 pages long, but it is filled with a philosophy of faith which is most beneficial to humans living in the mad rush of the twentieth century.

Odyssey

by Homer
Recommended by: Ed Davis,
Captain, U.S. Navy

The Latin classics, which I read in college, have remained at the very top of my list.

Executives

A Business And Its Beliefs

by Thomas J. Watson, Jr.
Recommended by: Howard W. Powell,
Professional/Management Development, IBM

Mr. Watson considers the remarkable growth of IBM, and attributes much of this success to a sound set of credos which serve as a foundation for the organization's policies and actions. He examines IBM's three basic beliefs—and states that "if an organization is to meet the challenges of a changing world, it must be prepared to change everything about itself except those beliefs as it moves through corporate life."

The author provides the reader with an insight into the character and personal convinctions of Thomas J. Watson, Sr., and describes how these values influenced the beliefs and policies of IBM. It is a look at the management philosophy which has made this organization one of America's most successful during the last sixty years.

Human Action:
A Treatise on Economics

by Ludwig Von Mises
Recommended by: Kenneth McFarland, CPAE,
Author, Educator, Professional Speaker

My favorite book is an economics volume by Ludwig Von Mises. He is the first of the economists to discover that economic laws do not operate in a vacuum. On the contrary, they are greatly affected by the political and social philosophy of the *people*. He knew economic laws won't work if the people won't. And he knew that economic laws can be repealed by governments. Not nullified; not proven false; just repealed, with all the disastrous results that follow such blundering.

The Letters of T. E. Lawrence

Edited by David Garnett
Recommended by: Ellen M. Putnam, CLU,
Insurance Exec., Recipient of the Natl. Assn. of
Life Underwriters' John Newton Russell Award

Years ago a dear friend and I enjoyed what Lawrence of Arabia wrote. He was a wonderful person and had much to give to everyone:

"It's my experience that the actual work or position or reward one has, doesn't have much effect on the inner being which is the most important thing for us to cultivate.

"If I have restored to the East some self-respect, a goal, ideals: if I have made the standard of rule of white over red more exigent, I have fitted those peoples in a degree for the new commonwealth in which the dominant races will forget their brute achievements, and white and red and yellow and brown and black will stand up together without side-glances in the service of the world."

                                                —T. E. Lawrence

"Part of Lawrence's success in helping others, grew out of his ability to keep his personal suffering apart from the daily congress of his life. He seems to have wrestled with his personal torments on his own time, and to have communicated them selectively in his writings, or in personal letters to friends."

                                                —John Mack, 1976

The Autobiography of Benjamin Franklin

Recommended by: John H. Rawley, Director of Human Resources, Hershey Foods Corporation

Benjamin Franklin's autobiography is a genuine classic. It should be on everyone's reading list:

Franklin's Thirteen Moral Virtues

1. TEMPERENCE. Eat not to dullness; drink not to elevation.
2. SILENCE. Speak not but what may benefit others.
3. ORDER. Let all things have their places; let each part of your business have its time.
4. RESOLUTION. Resolve to perform what you ought, perform without fail what you resolve.
5. FRUGALITY. Waste nothing.
6. INDUSTRY. Lose no time; be always employ'd in something useful; cut off all unnecessary actions.
7. SINCERITY. Use no hurtful deceit, think innocently and justly, and, if you speak, speak accordingly.
8. JUSTICE. Wrong none by doing injuries, or omitting the benefits that are your duty.
9. MODERATION. Avoid extremes.
10. CLEANLINESS. Tolerate no uncleanliness in body.
11. TRANQUILLITY. Be not disturbed at trifles.
12. CHASTITY. Rarely use venery but for health or offspring, never to dulness, weakness, or the injury of your own or another's pease or reputation.
13. HUMILITY. Imitate Jesus and Socrates.

Reminiscences

by Douglas MacArthur
Recommended by: L. J. Rowell, Jr., CLU
President, Provident Mutual

The book that has probably had the biggest influence on me is Douglas MacArthur's autobiography, *Reminiscences*. I periodically re-read his two great speeches, one which he made to Congress entitled, "Old Soldiers Never Die" and an even better one that he made to the cadets at West Point entitled, "The Long Grey Line."

Written in his own hand, and finished only weeks before his death, *Reminiscences* spans more than half a century of modern history.

Douglas MacArthur served under eight Presidents. He was honored as few men have been. His genius for command, and his ability to implement that command by strategy, stand as landmarks in military history. No man was ever so outspoken in his commitment to his troops or in his beliefs.

Never before has one soldier's life so completely reflected a nation's military history. After graduation from West Point with the highest average ever achieved by a cadet, MacArthur served in Vera Cruz during the Mexican uprisings and then as military attache in the Far East, where he first perceived Japanese aspirations for hegemony in the Orient. His courage in the trenches and his leadership of the famous Rainbow Division during the First World War were cited by General Pershing, who seven times awarded MacArthur the Silver Star.

Decade by decade, battlefield by battlefield, *Reminiscences* is a portrait of our most decorated military hero. It is the deeply moving final testament to a life of duty, honor and service.

Three Steps Forward, Two Steps Back

by Charles R. Swindoll
Recommended by: Ed Rush,
Referee, National Basketball Assn.

This book deals with deep human reactions to situations arising in personal relationships. I appreciated the chapter on being misunderstood:

"Few things are more difficult to live with than being misunderstood. Sometimes it's downright unbearable."

"When you are misunderstood, you have no defense. And have you noticed that when you are misunderstood, no matter how hard you try to correct the misunderstanding, it usually gets worse? You go fully loaded, ready to 'set them straight,' and all you do is dig yourself deeper! The harder you work, the worse it gets and the deeper it hurts. Its sting can be paralyzing."

"This past summer my wife and I went through one of the most painful times of our lives. Disarmed and defenseless, we got a firsthand, bitter taste of that painfully familiar paralyzing sting of humanity. We had done what was right, but we were misinterpreted and therefore maligned. Unfair criticism increased the pain and brought us, in tears, to our knees. I remembered a statement C. S. Lewis once made: 'God whispers to us in our pleasures, speaks in our conscience, but shouts in our pains: it is His megaphone to rouse a deaf world.'"

The Road to Serfdom

by Friedrich von Hayek
Recommended by: William Rusher
Publisher, National Review

"I had read and been powerfully impressed by Friedrich von Hayek's *The Road to Serfdom* not long after its publication in 1944. At Harvard Law School in 1947 I encountered it again, as required reading in Lon Luvois Fuller's wide-ranging course on jurisprudence. Also required was Barbara Wootton's formal book-length reply to Hayek, entitled *Freedom Under Planning* (Chapel Hill, 1945), and I recall being vividly impressed by how honestly, yet withal how unsuccessfully, the noted British socialist strove to refute Hayek.

As one reviewer remarked at the time, Hayek's assault on socialism and economic planning was 'no mere sortie from the castle: It is a full-scale attack, with horse, foot, and artillery.'"

(from *The Rise of the Right*)

"If we are to build a better world, we must have the courage to make a new start—even if that means some *reculer pour mieux sauter* . . . The young are right if they have little confidence in the ideas which rule most of their elders. But they are mistaken or misled when they believe that these are still the liberal ideas of the nineteenth century, which, in fact, the younger generation hardly knows. Though we neither can wish nor possess the power to go back to the reality of the nineteenth century, we have the opportunity to realize its ideals—and they were not mean . . . The guiding principle that a policy of freedom for the individual is the only truly progressive policy remains as true today as it was in the nineteenth century."

—von Hayek

Carl Sandburg and Heroes

There was such a thing as luck in life but if luck
didn't come your way it was up to you to step into
struggle and like it. I read Ouida's *Under Two Flags.*
The hero lost everything he had except a horse, lived
a dirty and bloody life as a fighting man, with never
a whimper. I read Olive Schreiner's *The Story of an
African Farm,* sad lives on nearly every page, and yet
a low music of singing stars and love too deep ever to
be lost. I believed there were lives far more bitter and
lonely than mine and they had fixed stars, dreams and
moonsheens, hopes and mysteries, worth looking at
during their struggles. I was groping.

"I read about the Spanish General Weyler and his
cruelties with the people of Cuba who wanted independence and a republic. I read about Gomez, Garcia,
Maceo, with their scrabbling little armies fighting
against Weyler. They became heroes to me.

Bernard Baruch and Heroes

Like all boys I had my childhood heroes. I was
brought up to believe that Robert E. Lee was the epit-
ome of all virtues. Father often quoted a maxim of Lee's
as a guide to my own conduct:

"Do your duty in all things. You could not do more.
You would not wish to do less."

Generals Beauregard, Stonewall Jackson, and Jeb
Stuart were other shining figures, as were Marion,
Sumter, and Picken from the Revolutionary War. Not
even George Washington loomed as large in my mind
as those soldiers of the swamp.

Ride the Wild Horses

by J. Wallace Hamilton
Recommended by: Robert Schuller,
Pastor, Author

The first influence that really impacted me was a book called *Ride the Wild Horses*. It remains one of the most influential books of my life. I was pastor of my first little church in a Chicago suburb when the book was given to me. It was based on the verse from the Bible, "The tongue of the wild horse." Dr. Hamilton showed how the uncontrolled word can destroy. But, harnessed, it becomes the most powerful and redeeming force in the world. The entire book treats the emotional forces that would be considered negative and turns them into positive surges. Angry? Frustrated? Upset because you are interrupted? A gambling instinct? All of these are forces that should not be destroyed within the life – but redeemed! Under the control of Christ and under the power of the Holy Spirit and wrapped in positive thinking, negative impulses and urges are to be seen as potentially powerful forces when channeled and controlled by Jesus Christ!

This book would set the tone for my self esteem theology. The ego. Is it to be destroyed? Is it a bad thing? Or is it a potentially powerful force for good in the human life?

The wild horses – the turbulent emotions, the stormy sessions of the soul – are to be viewed as challenges and opportunities in disguise! That's faith! That's riding the wild horses.

When I am reading a book, whether wise or silly, it seems to me to be alive and talking to me.

— Swift

Scaramouche

by Rafael Sabatini
Recommended by: William E. Simon
Former Secretary of the Treasury
President, Wesray Corp.

My all-time favorite book is one I read as a boy, *Scaramouche* by Rafael Sabatini. It's a great adventure story, and captures splendidly the times and spirit of the French Revolution. My favorite line in literature is its opening sentence; "He was born with a gift for laughter and a sense that all the world was mad." I sometimes fancy this could have been written about me, although it would be more accurate to say I acquired the sense that the world was mad after my years in Washington, rather than that I was born with it!

Scaramouche is one of Sabatini's most glorious tales of adventure and romance. It is the exciting story of Andre Louis Moreau, fugitive, strolling player, master of fence and wit, who gains fame and happiness at the point of the sword during the dangerous and romantic period of the French Revolution.

Forced to flee for his revolutionary activities in France, Andre joins a band of strolling players and takes the part of Scaramouche, a stock character of the French drama whose rogueries, witticisms, and adventures fit his own nature to perfection. He quickly becomes enmeshed in dangers, feuds, politics, and a romance so tense and profoundly absorbing you will be spellbound as you follow him through these crowded days of thrilling adventure.

The Richest Man in Babylon

by George Clason
Recommended by: Fred Smith,
Executive, Consultant, Author

This book is a story . . . A parable, the age-old best way to slip truth into our heart. In it, a rich man tells the secret of riches to a poor printer's laborer in exchange for his all-night effort getting out printing the rich man needs. At first the poor man felt cheated, for the advice was so simple, as most profitable advice is. However, the workman followed it and, while making some early mistakes, found the way to financial success. Even now, when I list the principles, I blush for their simplicity. Here are the simple rules I followed, as did the poor man in Babylon:

1. At least ten percent of all you make is yours to keep . . . pay yourself first.
2. Never invest with an amateur . . . a novice. He is prey to the pro.
3. Reinvest the interest you earn from all your savings: "Don't eat up your grandchildren."
4. Desire to acquire wealth through knowledge and association . . . knowledge of its way and association with those who are acquiring wealth.

I have found these principles moral. They violate no one's integrity. Openly desiring money is honorable, so long as one seeks money as a means to noble accomplishments, not to greed and self-aggrandizement. Money is, and has forever been, a trustworthy servant but a tyrannical master. The individual must decide which it will be.

The Constitution
of the United States of America

Recommended by: Raymond W. Smock,
Historian, U.S. House of Representatives

I am happy to be able to share a title that I have profited from reading on many occasions. I am not sure that what I suggest precisely fits the category of a book, but I think all will agree with me that The Constitution of the United States of America is pretty powerful reading.

This brief but profound document is the hallmark of our free society, and establishes the framework for governing our great democracy. While many volumes of interpretation and case law surround and expand the document itself, there is so much that can be learned about what it means to be an American from a reading of the basic document itself and the 26 amendments that accompany it. As we approach the 200th anniversary of the U.S. Constitution I cannot think of a single book, article, or document that I would recommend more highly than the Constitution itself.

A man who has any relish for fine writing either discovers new beauties, or receives stronger impressions, from the masterly strokes of a great author every time he peruses him; besides that he naturally wears himself into the same manner of speaking and thinking.

–Addison: *Spectator*, No. 409

Life Is Tremendous

by Charles "T" Jones
Recommended by: Louis Sportelli, D.C.

One of the greatest books to ever come across my path was *Life Is Tremendous* by Charles "T" Jones. I have given more than 500 of these books to patients and friends because of the humorous style. It is packed with the wisdom of the ages. *Life Is Tremendous* allows you to laugh at yourself, pray for problems, and learn how to establish the basic fundamentals of success . . . as a person.

Books are the SILVER of the mind. If left on the shelf, they tarnish; but if read, they give your mind the glitter of new ideas and the shine of a renewed motivation to solve the challenges of life and success.

When a book like *Life Is Tremendous* is experienced and then shared, the benefits are two-fold. First to the receiver in new knowledge and attitude, and secondly to the giver in knowing they have touched a person's life.

Laughter is what *Life Is Tremendous* promotes, along with an inspection of one's attitude. Perhaps the best way to describe what occurs was said by Victor Hugo: "I like the laughter that opens the lips and the heart, that shows at the same time pearls and the soul."

The first time I read an excellent book, it is to me just as if I had gained a new friend. When I read over a book I have perused before, it resembles the meeting with an old one.

— Oliver Goldsmith

The Knowledge of the Holy

by A. W. Tozer
Recommended by: Walter A. Stenger
President, Investment Timing Services, Inc.

In his book, *The Knowledge of the Holy,* A. W. Tozer presents a clear, simple, and interesting discussion of God's attributes. He feels that men today need to cherish loftier ideas of God, and should let these ideas determine their daily thoughts and life.

On "The Self-Sufficiency of God," Dr. Tozer states, "Were all human beings suddenly to become blind, still the sun would shine by day and the stars by night, for these owe nothing to the millions who benefit from their light. So, were every man on earth to become atheist, it could not affect God in any way. He is what He is in Himself without regard to any other. To believe in Him adds nothing to His perfections; to doubt Him takes nothing away.

"What peace it brings to the Christian's heart to realize that our Heavenly Father never differs from Himself. In coming to Him at any time, we need not wonder whether we shall find Him in a receptive mood. He is always receptive to misery and need, as well as to love and faith. He does not keep office hours nor set aside periods when He will see no one. Neither does He change His mind about anything."

As a businessman overseeing a multi-million dollar operation, I have found this book to be a constant source of truth which helps to keep my thinking about God and about my fellow man correct. The pages of this book have become well-worn these last twenty-two years.

W. Clement Stone & A Book

(From *The Success System That Never Fails*)

It was in 1937 that I was given the strangest book ever written.

Morris Pickus, a well-known sales executive and sales counselor, was at that time selling a book to sales organizations. When he endeavored to get me to purchase this book for my sales force, I turned him down, for as I paged through it, I knew for a certainty it was something I didn't want.

When Morris Pickus lost the sale, he did something that changed the course of my life. He gave me another book, *Think and Grow Rich,* in which he had inscribed a personal note of inspiration. When I read *Think and Grow Rich,* its philosophy coincided with my own in so many respects that I, too, started the habit of helping others by giving them inspirational self-help books. The one principle that particularly helped me was Napoleon Hill's mastermind principle—two or more persons working together in harmony toward a common goal. It made me realize that I could employ others to do much of the work that I was doing, and thus I would have more time for additional activities.

I shall never be able to repay him for the help I received from the book he gave me.

I did think—and grow rich. Any of my sales representatives who were willing to relate, assimilate, and use the principles—they, too, thought and grew rich. Each of them received the book from me.

The Effective Executive

by Peter Drucker
Recommended by: Frank E. Sullivan, OLU
President, Mutual Benefit Life

If I got nothing more from Peter Drucker's *The Effective Executive* than the one phrase: "Efficiency is doing things right—Effectiveness is doing the right things right," I would feel the time spent reading and studying the book was well worth it.

But, I got many other excellent ideas from this valuable part of my library.

I have six Vice Presidents or Senior Vice Presidents reporting to me. We compose our "Insurance Operations Committee" and we meet monthly. One hour of our meeting is devoted to a "Book Review" with a different member of the committee being responsible for moderating a session each month. Some time back we reviewed *The Effective Executive*. Here are some of the good ideas we got from Drucker:

"To be effective is the job of the executive."

"Intelligence, imagination and knowledge are essential resources, but only effectiveness converts them into results."

"The only resource in respect to which America can possibly have a competitive advantage is education."

"Productivity for the knowledge worker means the ability to get the right things done. It means effectiveness."

"Knowledge work is not defined by Quantity. It is defined by results."

Excellence in Leadership

by Frank Goble
Recommended by: *Rev. Charles Swindoll,*
Pastor, Author, Fullerton, California

A book I have profited by is *Excellence in Leadership*.
Here are a few quotes which will help explain why:

"Moses chose able men out of all Israel, and made
them heads over the people, rulers of thousands, of
hundreds, of fifties, and of tens." (Exodus 18:25)

"'It is not technology itself which succeeds; it is
trained and motivated man who applies technology
with judgement and creativity. It is man who must
assume responsibility, plan new approaches, take risks,
and make difficult decisions.'–Paul Thayer, President,
LTV Aerospace Corp."

"H. Ross Perot, whose success as president of Elec-
tronic Data Systems (EDS) was so spectacular that
Fortune dubbed him the fastest, richest Texan ever, says
that the careful selection of employees is one of his
major rules for success. EDS will sometimes interview
400 applicants to find one new employee."

"J. P. Morgan, who knew the value of a dollar better
than most, once said, 'I will pay more for the ability
of a man to lead others than for any other asset.' What
is it that makes some people so successful in their
human relations while others just as intelligent fail? Isn't
it precisely the qualities described above–ambition,
persistence, courage, faith, integrity, sense of justice,
objectivity, flexibility, self-discipline, decisiveness? Isn't
it a series of related attitudes one holds toward others?
Consideration, cooperation, humility, and loyalty? Isn't
it . . . the ability to communicate? But isn't it also
something more basic than all of these things–self-
respect and self-confidence?"

The Greatest Success in the World

by Og Mandino
Recommended by: Claude I. Taylor,
CEO, Air Canada

One of the most interesting "little books" I have read recently is Og Mandino's *The Greatest Success in the World*. One of the parts that impressed me was his Tenth Commandment for success: "Thou Must Never Strive to Be Anything But Thyself":

"Consider the plants and the animals of the field, how they live. Does a cotton plant bear even one apple? Does a pomegranate tree ever produce an orange? Does a lion attempt to fly?"

"Only man, of all living things, foolishly strives to be other than what he was intended to be until life marks him a misfit. Misfits are the failures of the world, always chasing after a more fruitful career they will never find unless they look behind them."

"You cannot choose your calling. Your calling chooses you. You have been blessed with special skills that are yours alone. Use them, whatever they may be, and forget about wearing another's hat. A talented chariot driver can win gold and renown with his skills. Let him pick figs and he would starve."

"No one can take your place. Realize this and be yourself. You have no obligation to succeed. You have only the obligation to be true to yourself."

In Search of Excellence

by Thomas J. Peters and Robert H. Waterman Jr.
Recommended by: Ronald Terry,
Chairman, First Tennessee National Corp.

In Search of Excellence, by Thomas J. Peters and Robert H. Waterman Jr., explains the traits and patterns shared by companies which have demonstrated high levels of success and shows how the most successful organizations exemplify the behavior patterns they had when they were small companies. Such businesses encourage innovation, decentralize operations, stress action and focus on a few simple values.

The most interesting part of the study for me, however, was how simple, consistent communication throughout an organization is a strategy for focusing commitment on the company's values. By focusing on a few specific values, a company can develop an image which distinguishes it from competitors throughout the years. Peters and Waterman explain that communicating values is the responsibility of every employee, and the communication must be repeated frequently. To establish values and to be identified with them, the simple messages must be known and exemplified at all levels of the organization day-to-day, year-to-year, through various mediums.

We are now in want of an art to teach how books are to be read rather than to read them. Such an art is practicable.

— Disraeli

Margaret Thatcher & Books

Prime Minister, England

The local librarian, Peter Willard, recalls that young Margaret used to appear at the library to collect "armfuls of books for him every week." Those books, mostly biographies and studies of current affairs were thoroughly discussed at home. Roberts fancied himself a keen student of world events, and he insisted that his daughters share his interest. They did, particularly Margaret. Madeline Hellaby, a schoolmate of young Margaret's during World War II, tells the story of how, during a classroom "discussion of an RAF bombing raid in Europe, she knew where the place of the raid was and no one else did. The mistress asked how, and she said, 'Any time a bombing raid is mentioned on the wireless, we get the atlas out and put a pin in to mark the location.'"

Alfred Roberts did more than just discuss events with his daughters. He had keenly-held political beliefs and he discussed those too. As one might expect of a self-made man blessed with considerable personal initiative and individual enterprise, he had absolutely no sympathy for the growing trade union movement in prewar Britain.

For the Robertses, Sunday was a day of prayer and study—and nothing else. The shop was closed and going to the movies was out of the question, even Sunday newspapers were barred from the household. The family was up for breakfast at eight a.m. and at ten the girls were sent off to Sunday school. They would join their parents for the morning service at eleven, return to Sunday school in the afternoon, and then attend another church service at six in the evening.

—Allan H. Mayer

The Power of Positive Thinking

by Dr. Norman Vincent Peale
Recommended by: R. David Thomas,
Founder & Chairman of the Board,
Wendy's International, Inc.

Of the many great books I have read, the most inspiring to me is *The Power of Positive Thinking,* by Dr. Norman Vincent Peale.

The book is both very inspirational and highly motivating. It touches upon every aspect for successful living, such as believing in yourself and replacing negative thoughts with positive ones. It provides a practical guide for everyday living:

"BELIEVE IN YOURSELF! Have faith in your abilities! Without a humble but reasonable confidence in your own powers you cannot be successful or happy. But with sound self-confidence you can succeed. A sense of inferiority and inadequacy interferes with the attainment of your hopes, but self-confidence leads to self-realization and successful achievement. Because of the importance of this mental attitude, this book will help you believe in yourself and release your inner powers.

"It is appalling to realize the number of pathetic people who are hampered and made miserable by the malady popularly called the inferiority complex. But you need not suffer from this trouble. When proper steps are taken, it can be overcome. You can develop creative faith in yourself—faith, that is justified."

The Rivers Ran East

by Leanord Clark
Recommended by: Dr. Clay Thompson, D.C.,
Educator

Leanord Clark is one of the few explorers who has given an account of a trip to the head waters of the mighty Amazon, in South America. With no backing by anyone and with limited capital ($1000), he tackled an almost impossible journey in search of the gold at El Dorado.

His contacts with the various tribes of Indians who had never seen a white man will send chills up your spine.

If it was not for the fact that many of the stories in this book have been verified by unimpeachable sources, it would appear to be fantasy!

From the foreword:

"I am a Peruvian, a veteran resident of the jungle. I have spent a quarter of a century of my life on the main trunk rivers of the Amazonic regions. Adventure as I personally know, is not the mark of incompetency, as many experts would have us believe. It is a barometer showing just how far into the true unknown (of the Amazon regions at any rate) the explorer has been able to go. Clark cuts into ribbons all tactical methods of advancing. He does not cover his rear against the attack of the savages. He has no consideration for bringing up supplies and protection to that point of zero where it is a calculated 99% risk to advance further before turning back. He just goes!

"The calculated risks and dangers, accent the readability and permanent value of his book."

Hand Me Another Brick

by Charles Swindoll
Recommended by: Andre Thornton,
Baseball Player, Cleveland Indians

A book which I thought was excellent and one that can be applied to our lives was *Hand Me Another Brick*, by Charles Swindoll. There are many books which have been a blessing to me and this certainly has been one of them.

"If happiness were a disease, none other would be more contagious. If you laugh often, if you're having fun in life, if you're never very far from a smile, you'll have no trouble infecting people and making friends. People who really enjoy life are always, *always* in demand. They are unbelievably infectious!

"Remember the words in Proverbs 17:22: 'a joyful heart is good medicine'? Well, there's another verse you may not have found which states, 'A joyful heart makes a cheerful face, but when the heart is sad, the spirit is broken' (Prov. 15:13). Isn't that the truth! It's the individual who smiles and sings his way through life whom people want to be around. I repeat, a joyful heart is contagious. And it fits any scene, no matter how bad the circumstances.

"I understand that Charles Haddon Spurgeon was once chided for injecting a fair amount of humor into his preaching. With a twinkle in his eye, he replied, 'If only you knew how much I hold back, you would commend me.'"

Harry S. Truman and Books

Harry Truman always said . . . that a man could do anything he set his mind to . . . he volunteered once to give me a list of about ten or so books that I ought to read . . . I can remember that it included Plutarch's *Lives*. And Caesar's *Commentaries*. And Benjamin Franklin's *Autobiography*. He used to say, "Al, you'll find a good deal in there about how to make use of every minute of your day and a lot of horse sense about people." And he was always talking about the Roman lawgivers. He knew all about them. And he had read all of Gibbon's *Decline and Fall of the Roman Empire* several times . . . he was always reading two or three books at a time and always making notes in the margins, especially in history books . . .

He told me to read a book called *Bunker Bean* and one called *Missouri's Struggle for Statehood*. The Bible. I remember he said even back then that the King James Version was the best and that he doubted it could be improved on . . . Plato's *Republic*. Shakespeare. He said I'd have to read all of Shakespeare, but he recommended *Hamlet* and *Lear* and *Othello* in particular, and the sonnets.

He recommended to me the complete works of Robert Burns, which he was always reading himself. And Byron. All of Byron, too, I believe, although his favorite was *Childe Harold* . . . There was a book called *Fifteen Decisive Battles of the World*. Harry Truman felt that you had to understand war to understand mankind.

—Judge Albert A. Ridge

The Peloponnesian War

by Thucydides (471–400 B.C.)
Recommended by: Ted Turner
President, Turner Broadcasting System

"The absence of romance in my history will, I fear, detract somewhat from its interest; but if it be judged useful by those inquirers who desire an exact knowledge of the past as an aid to the interpretation of the future, which in the course of human things must resemble if it does not reflect it, I shall be content. In fine, I have written my work, not as an essay which is to win the applause of the moment, but as a possession for all time."

"Thus every form of iniquity took root in the Hellenic countries by reason of the troubles. The ancient simplicity into which honour so largely entered was laughed down and disappeared; and society became divided into camps in which no man trusted his fellow . . . In the confusion into which life was now thrown in the cities, human nature, always rebelling against the law and now its master, gladly showed itself ungoverned in passion, above respect for justice, and the enemy of all superiority."

"As between neighbors generally, freedom means simply a determination to hold one's own; and with neighbors like these, who are trying to enslave near and far alike, there is nothing for it but to fight it out to the last."

The choice of books, like that of friends, is a serious duty. We are as responsible for what we read as what we do.

—John Lubbock

The Practice of Management

by Peter F. Drucker
Recommended by: Jack Twyman,
Chairman, Pres. & CEO, Super Food Services

I had the privilege of being in Mr. Drucker's audience on a number of occasions. When I have an opportunity to daydream, I always go back to his book and find so many rational and logical thoughts that often times we in business overlook due to the press of day-to-day business. They have been a great source of inspiration for me, and a source of knowledge for anyone who cares to take the time and effort to read the works of this outstanding business philosopher:

"Management must always, in every decision and action, put economic performance first. It can only justify its existence and its authority by the economic results it produces.

". . . management – almost alone – has to live always in both present and future . . . management must keep the enterprise successful and profitable in the present – or else there will be no enterprise left to enjoy the future. It must simultaneously make the enterprise capable of growing and prospering, or at least of surviving in the future . . .

"It is the first duty of a business to survive. The guiding principle of business economics, in other words, is not the maximization of profits; it is the avoidance of loss. Business enterprise must produce the premium to cover the risks inevitably involved in its operation."

Great Thoughts About Books

Knowledge should be a compound of what we derive from books, and what we extract, by our observation, from the living world around us. Both of these are necessary to the well-informed man; and, of the two, the last is, by far, the most useful for the practical purposes of life. The man who can combine the teachings of books with strong and close observation of life, deserves the name of a well-informed man, and presents a model worthy of imitation.

—Sir Thomas Lipton

An unread man has only to read a very few of the great representative novels to find where he stands, what his tastes are likely to be, and what it is that he is looking for in books. A living library is not to be deliberately made. You cannot plan it out on paper and then buy it en bloc. Of course you can make a collection of books in that way, but a collection of books is not a library. A bookstore is a collection of books, but it is not a library. A library is an organism developing side by side with the mind and character of its owner. It is the house of his spirit and is thus furnished progressively in accordance with the progress of his mental life.

—Richard Le Gallienne

True books have been written in all ages by their greatest men; by great leaders, great statesmen, and great thinkers. These are all of your choice, and life is short. Will you jostle with the common crowd, for entree here and audience there, when all the while this eternal court is open to you, with its society as the world, multitudinous as its day, the chosen and the mighty of every time and place?

—John Ruskin

Man builds no structure which outlives a book.

—E. F. Ware

Tough Minded Faith
For Tender Hearted People
by Robert H. Schuller
Recommended by: Venita Van Caspel,
President, VanCaspel & Co.

"FAITH IS . . . Embracing God's grace."
"Grace is the most beautiful word in the English language. Nothing is more valuable than a gift that is given when you don't deserve it—

- love before you've earned it.
- credit when it is not justified.

"The hardest task in the world is for an honorable person to accept something he has not earned. This explains why people are extremely reticent and resistant to accepting the gospel of Jesus Christ, salvation by the grace of God.

"Today make one of the greatest leaps of faith that is possible! Embrace God's grace. Accept His understanding and forgiveness. Trust Him not only to cleanse you of sin and negativity but to inspire you to treat other persons the same way.

"You suddenly realize that you are *forgiven not through the good works you do, but to do good works.*"

Man's Search for Meaning

by Viktor Frankl
Recommended by: Marilyn Van Derbur, CPAE
Miss America, Radio and TV Personality

It is rare for me to read a book twice. I felt a need to read *Man's Search for Meaning* a third time because Viktor Frankl answers unanswerable questions. I wanted to have his thoughts indelibly imprinted in my mind.

More than once in an airport or on a plane I have wanted to say to a stranger, "Let me share this paragraph with you . . . and this one . . . just one more!"

What if everything material were abruptly taken from us and we were left without a penny, without a home, ample food . . . even the clothes on our bodies? How would we react?

Then, if everyone we held dear were taken from us: our loved ones . . . not just our mates, children, parents, aunts, uncles, and cousins, but also our friends? And if they were all killed in a relatively short time, would we have a meaningful reason to live?

Finally if we lost our freedom and were put in a prison camp where death was imminent everyday, every hour, would we choose to live? Until death, how would we bear up under the pressure?

Having survived three years at Auschwitz and other Nazi prison camps, Viktor Frankl provides answers that, if they are not new, certainly seemed to be in the way he focused his experience into ideas that influence my thinking, my everyday life.

Me: The Narcissistic American

By Aaron Stern, M.D.
Recommended by: Denis E. Waitley
Author, President, Denis E. Waitley, Inc.

In a penetrating chapter on marriage, Dr. Stern points out, "love always begins as an illusion," which a man and woman create naturally during courtship. "By falling in love with that image of a person before we can know his true substance, we assign him qualities we want to believe he has. In that way we can think of the person in terms that enchance our own lives."

Stern's perceptions are laser accurate. Nearly all of us enter our romantic relationship expecting the other person to provide some kind of magic. Our physical attraction to our mate certainly is filled with this kind of expectation. And so we spend our courtship trying to win the other person over to our side as we play up our most flattering features. Every courtship has its elements of adolescent coltishness and selfishness. It is perfectly natural and adds spice to the relationship.

Stern goes on to share one of the richest understandings of what marriage should be I have ever encountered. What Stern seems to say is that a little narcissism never hurt any marriage, but he is careful to qualify what he means by "a little." He believes every marriage needs some narcissistic love as the spice to keep romance alive. But he cautions: "Spice is only a seasoning added to a much larger mass of food for flavor; too much ruins the taste of the food that it was intended to improve. Such is the nature of narcissistic love. Small amounts enhance the quality of loving within a marriage. Too much will destroy the marriage itself."

Booker T. Washington & Books

Portia Pitman, Daughter

When I was a girl at school, my father was constantly sending books to me. Among these were *Aesop's Fables, Stories from the Greeks, Grimms' Fairy Tales,* and *The Knights of the Round Table.* He also made special arrangements for me to have physical exercises for health in Boston. He was the most thoughtful person I ever knew in my life. He was very affectionate and sympathetic. He used to help me with mathematics, which I hated. Once he gave me a really terrible scolding and then came back later and was very penitent for having been so severe. We never at home began the day without prayer, and we closed the day with prayer in the evening. He read the Bible to us at breakfast each day and prayed; that was never missed. Really he prayed all the time. His faith built Tuskegee. In all his travels he always carried Shakespeare with him and read constantly. Repeatedly his speeches showed how he brooded over his Shakespeare until the inner meaning of the scenes saturated his spirit.

While you converse with lords and dukes, I have their betters here – my books.

—Thomas Sheridan

The Gulag Archipelago

by Aleksandr Solzhenitsyn
Recommended by: R. Douglas Wead,
Author, Professional Speaker

Certainly one of the world's greatest books is *The Gulag Archipelago*. All the great philosophical issues are put to the test. What is so inspiring to me is that Alexander Solzhenitsyn not only survived the Soviet system, he triumphed over it. His faith in God and even in his fellow man remained intact. While the Soviet colonial empire is stronger and more powerful than ever, one could make a good case that Solzhenitsyn's book marked the end of the Western intellectual romantization of a world-wide socialist revolution. If Solzhenitsyn can triumph over such incredible injustice and inconsistency, maybe I can survive the minor injustices and inconsistencies I must face daily.

"So many deep historians have written so many clever books – and still they have not learned how to predict those mysterious conflagrations of the human spirit, to detect the mysterious springs of a social explosion, nor even to explain them in retrospect. Sometimes you can stuff bundle after bundle of burning tow under the logs, and they will not take. Yet up above, a solitary little spark flies out of the chimney and the whole village is reduced to ashes."

"When a train carries you in the wrong direction and you decide to jump off, you have to jump with the motion of the train, and not against it. The inertial force of history is just as hard to resist."

Why Am I Afraid to Tell You Who I Am?

by John Powell
Recommended by: Dennis Wholey,
Host/LateNight America (PBS)

Father Powell writes about the human spirit, our vision of ourselves and the world, what it means to be fully alive, and how to say yes to life.

The book has sold several million copies. His thesis is that we all wear masks and play games to protect ourselves in order to be accepted. He points out that every human being has a real need to be listened to, to be taken seriously, and to be understood. No one, he writes, can develop freely without feeling understood by at least one person.

He goes on to say that self-revelation is the key to being understood and being accepted, but we are afraid to reveal ourselves for fear of rejection.

"I am afraid to tell you who I am because if I tell you who I am, you may not like who I am and it's all that I have." As you can see from that one sentence, Father Powell has something very important to offer us in our quest for self knowledge and growth.

Father Powell examines the fears, the doubts, the scars and the pains we all have and the roles we play and the masks we wear. He encourages us to take risks, open up, be ourselves, and experience love.

Why Am I Afraid to Tell You Who I Am? is a liberating experience. It helped me. It still does. Growth continues.

Autobiography of God

by Lloyd John Ogilvie
Recommended by: Skip Wilkins, Speaker,
Author, Gold Medalist, Olympics for the Disabled

The impact of the parables in *Autobiography of God* was tremendous. I still return to it today for more teaching and understanding. Oglivie's writing style captivates me. He is not only informative but very descriptive.

A chapter I have shared with many audiences is, "The Treasure Is You." This parable concerns knowing and doing the will of God. Its teaching is important today, with all the pressures of the world, the personal obstacles we must deal with, and the inferiority complexes against which many people struggle daily.

"The kingdom of heaven is like a treasure hidden in a field, which a man found and hid; and from joy over it he goes and sells all that he has, and buys the field" (Matt. 13:44).

"Again, the kingdom of heaven is like a merchant seeking fine pearls, and upon finding the one pearl of great value, he went and sold all that he had, and bought it" (Matt. 13:45,46).

Our first response is, "What means that much to us? What would we value as highly as a treasure or pearl? Does God and His kingdom?" When we look at the parable again, we see it tells us about the purpose of Jesus' passion and the passionate purpose He unleashes in our lives.

Jesus is saying, "You are the treasure! You are the pearl of great prize. I have found you." He is the plowman, the merchantman. God with us is saying, "You are everything to me! No cost is too high!"

Love Life For Every Married Couple

by Dr. Ed Wheat
Recommended by: Pat Williams, VP & General
Manager, Philadelphia 76ers Basketball Club

My wife bought a book (she was always buying books on marriage and family, reading and underlining in red, then leaving them where I'd find them) and left it on my nightstand. During a sleepless night, I miraculously happened to pick it up. Turning to the back cover, I read a quote to the effect that this was absolutely the best, most practical, helpful book on marriage ever written. The quote was from Charles Swindoll, one of my favorite writers and speakers. I turned the book over and read *Love Life For Every Married Couple*, by Dr. Ed Wheat. Like a thirsty man in the desert, I began to drink in the cool water of the words written by this man. Night after night, through teary eyes I discovered all the areas where I had gone wrong, ultimately realizing the root of the problem. I had never truly committed myself to my wife. I *loved* her, but didn't know the first principle about *loving* her. It was almost like trying to slam dunk a basketball without knowing how to dribble or pass the ball.

If you are contemplating divorce or separation; if you are living together but not enjoying it; if you think there must be more; or, if you think your marriage is *good*, this book is for you! No matter the state of your marriage, it will only improve. Believe me, I'll never stop applying Dr. Wheat's Biblical principles – I like it too much this way!

American Caesar

by William Manchester
Recommended by: W.C. Willis, Jr.,
President, Jenos

Major General Charles T. Menoher was quoted as saying, "MacArthur is the bloodiest fighting man in this army. I am afraid we are going to lose him sometime, for there is no risk of battle that any soldier is called upon to take that he is not liable to look up and see MacArthur at his side."

This statement has been of particular importance to me because I have always handled my personal and corporate life through "Leading by example." I am a strong believer that everything is a team effort and that every team member must be participating to his full capacity . . . no prima donnas.

The above reference to MacArthur is a classic example describing a man willing to do everything that he is asking his subordinates to do, rather than falling back on the cliche: "Do as I say, not as I do."

Furthermore, MacArthur clearly demonstrated that it is important not to have preconceived notions and not to decide on an answer before a question is asked. One should be willing to seize opportunities even if there are risks.

I am a very firm believer that both in my personal life and in the way I manage my business, one must be willing to keep an open mind, assess the situation (both risks and rewards), then seize the opportunity. People who go into situations with closed minds and a lack of conviction to seize opportunities will never succeed . . . in anything!

The Mature Mind

by Dr. Harry Overstreet
Recommended by: Larry Wilson, CPAE,
President, Wilson Learning Corp.

Dr. Harry Overstreet wrote a book that not only turned me on, it turned me inside out. It's called *The Mature Mind*.

Set humanness is the knowledge-ignorance theory. The idea here is that once people become smart, that is, filled with "book learning," they'll automatically see right from wrong and behave in a way that reflects the right and rejects the wrong.

Dr. Overstreet says: "By and large, Americans have an enormous faith in education . . . even when they have not defined it. Through this faith they have expressed both their feeling that things are sure to become better, and their generous feeling that most people are a pretty good lot. Even though they may, in their moments of anger, or in their area of authority, act out the goodness-badness theory, they tend in their more relaxed moments, and in their appraisal of life in general, to feel that if only people can be enough educated in the knowledge of the what, why and how of things, all will be right with the world."

He goes on to say, "Yet, when we regard the curious perversities to be found among many 'educated' adults, self-absorptions, pettiness, fears, egotisms, prejudices, dogmatisms, pedantries . . . we are forced to wonder whether the dispelling of ignorance is anything more than the merest beginning of wisdom, not its achievement."

How I Raised Myself From Failure To Success In Selling

by Frank Bettger
Recommended by: Thomas J. Wolff, CLU,
Insurance Exec., Recipient of the National Assn.
of Life Underwriters' John Newton Russell Award

The book I would like people to consider is Frank Bettger's immortal *How I Raised Myself From Failure To Success In Selling.* This book has had a dramatic affect on my life and on more sales people than any other. Here are a few great quotes from it:

"I don't think anybody is cut out to be a salesman or anything else. I think we've got to cut ourselves out to be whatever we want to be."

"It is surprising how much I get done when I take enough time for planning and it is perfectly amazing how little I get done without it."

"One of the greatest satisfactions in life comes from getting things done and knowing you have done them to the best of your ability."

"The most important secret of salesmanship is to find out what the other fellow wants, then help him find the best way to get it."

"Enthusiasm is the highest paid quality on earth."

Faith (Volume 2)

by Gabriel Heatter
Recommended by: Robert L. Woods, CLU,
Insurance Exec., Recipient of the National Assn.
of Life Underwriters' John Newton Russell Award

It is difficult, if not impossible, to recommend a book as being the most outstanding I have ever read. After all, the contents of a given book relate to a given area or to certain areas of our living, and one book can't cover all areas.

However, a little book of essays published in 1937 has long had a great impact on my life, and on those with whom I have shared some of the thoughts in both individual conversations and group presentations.

Here is just one of the important thoughts contained in the book. The thought is titled "Up-Stream and Down":

"Up-stream is where the rocks and boulders are. Where the rapids run. And the climb is hard and high. A man can't float as he can going downstream. But up-stream is the only trip worthwhile if you are travelling the river called Life.

"Yes, there are scars and scrapes and scratches which go deep and hurt. But the man who is going up-stream knows the exhilaration of battle and the exaltation of spirit which down-stream never provides.

"If you want to float and coast along – down-stream is your highway, and you will find lots of company. But if you are going anywhere at all and really want to get there – Up-stream is your road. And this is where you will find all the elbow room a man will ever need."

Psycho-Cybernetics

by Maxwell Maltz
Recommended by: Jim Young, Head Football
Coach, U.S. Military Academy, West Point

I would have to say that the book that had the most influence on my life would be *Psycho-Cybernetics* by Maxwell Maltz. It was the first book to open my eyes to the proper use of our minds.

Since then, I have read many, many books that have been helpful to me but I would have to say that this book would be the main one.

"You can mentally accept and digest these gradual doses of optimism and faith. After having thought of the desired end result as a definite 'possibility' – begin to imagine what the desirable outcome would be like. Go over these mental pictures and delineate details and refinements. Play them over and over to yourself. As your mental images become more detailed, as they are repeated over and over again – you will find that once more *appropriate feelings* are beginning to manifest themselves, just as if the favorable outcome had already happened. This time the appropriate feelings will be those of faith, self-confidence, courage – or all wrapped up into one package, "'That Winning Feeling.'"

Geri

by Geri Jewell
Recommended by: Robbie Zastavny,
1977 March of Dimes Poster Child

When I was watching "Facts of Life" on television, I was introduced to Geri Jewell, who has cerebral palsy. Later I had a chance to meet her in person. After meeting her, I read her book, *Geri*. In the book, she says, "Because of being disabled I have always been some kind of challenge to someone, especially myself. There is a little voice inside me that keeps telling me I've got to be as good as, if not better than, the next. I guess, as a result, I tend to be too hard on myself. But I like that better than fear of failure."

Sometimes when you are younger you think that because you are handicapped you cannot do anything. But when I read about Geri Jewell and realized how she was inspired, it helped me to know that I, too, can set a goal and achieve it.

The Heart Does Not Speak English

by William B. McGrath, M.D.
Recommended by: Zig Ziglar, CPAE,
Author, Executive

The Heart Does Not Speak English is a compilation of essays primarily dealing with human problems and their solutions. The approach to problem-solving is from a logical, scientific, Christian point of view. The examples Dr. McGrath uses are clear, concise and understandable. Anyone who reads *The Heart Does Not Speak English*, and takes the messages to heart, will be a better person as a result.

One example: Dr. McGrath points out that from the age of five to adolescence, children go through a latency period. During this time, little boys need to learn how to get along with other little boys by playing little boy games. Little girls need to learn how to get along with other little girls and play little girl games. To artificially stimulate a child sexually, whether via the media, sex education, or family involvements, does the child irreparable damage. It speeds them into adolescence, but tragically delays – sometimes permanently – their entrance into a normal adult life. The incredible number of twenty-five and thirty-year-olds in our society today who are not making it and have to return home or receive support from their parents, lends testimony to what Dr. McGrath is saying. The book is small but potent.

Great Thoughts
On
Reading

The Importance of Reading

by J. C. Penney

The reading of good books is one of the most helpful ways in which young people can develop themselves. One of the saddest mistakes I made in years gone by was utter neglect of reading. I realize now what I have missed by not having read and studied more.

I should like to say to the young men in particular that it is a splendid thing to make money, but it is a greater thing to make a good way of life. If they will devote some time each day to reading the best books they can find they will derive a lasting benefit throughout their lives.

To read good books casually will not suffice. One must study every sentence and make sure of its full message. Good writers do not intend that we should get their full meaning without effort. They expect us to dig just as one is compelled to dig for gold. Gold, you know, is not generally found in large openings, but in tiny veins. The ore must be subjected to a white heat in order to get the pure gold. So remember this when you read.

Young men and women who are seeking to learn all they can, have minds capable of receiving and retaining new impressions. There is nothing that will strengthen the mind, broaden the vision, enrich the soul, like the reading of good books. One can find or make no better friend than a good book.

Books: Read 'em and Reap The Benefits

by Abigail Van Buren

If I could give young people one piece of advice, it would be, read, read, read!

Reading will open up new worlds, real and imagined. Read for information, read for pleasure, read for inspiration.

Our libraries contain a wealth of information and entertainment, and it's all yours – as much as you want – free for the taking.

The person who DOES NOT read has no advantage over the person who CANNOT READ.

I encourage parents to read to their very young children. This loving act will create a bond of closeness between parent and child as well as make the child aware of the buried treasures that can be found in books.

Let me share with you the closing paragraph from one of my favorite poems, "The Reading Mother" by Strickland Gillilan:

"You may have tangible wealth untold;
"Caskets of jewels and coffers of gold.

"Richer than I you can never be –
"I had a mother who read to me."

Thoughts About Reading

Reading is to the mind what exercise is to the body.
— Richard Steele

The wisdom of the wise and the experience of the ages are perpetuated by quotation.
— Benjamin Disraeli

He is a rich man who can avail himself of all men's faculties.
— Ralph Waldo Emerson

Cultivation is necessary to the mind as food is to the body.
— Cicero

When we read we may not only be kings and live in palaces, but, what is far better, we may transport ourselves to the mountains or the seashore, and visit the most beautiful parts of the earth, without fatigue, inconvenience, or expense.
— John Lubbock

To read without reflecting is like eating without digesting.
— Burke

"Much, Not Many"

Charles Haddon Spurgeon
1834–1892

Books on the brain cause disease. Get the book into the brain, and you will grow. In Disraeli's "Curiosities of Literature" there is an invective of Lucian upon those men who boast of possessing large libraries, which they either never read or never profit by. He begins by comparing such a person to a pilot who has never learned the art of navigation, or a cripple who wears embroidered slippers but cannot stand upright in them. Then he exclaims, "Why do you buy so many books? You have no hair, and you purchase a comb; you are blind, and you must need buy a fine mirror; you are deaf, and you will have the best musical instrument!" – a very well deserved rebuke to those who think that the possession of books will secure them learning. A measure of that temptation happens to us all; for do we not feel wiser after we have spent an hour or two in a bookseller's shop? A man might as well think himself richer for having inspected the vaults of the Bank of England. In reading books let your motto be, "MUCH, NOT MANY." Think as well as read, and keep the thinking always proportionate to the reading, and your small library will not be a great misfortune.

Thoughts About Reading

Reading maketh a full man, conference a ready man, and writing an exact man.

—Francis Bacon

The greatest part of a writer's time is spent in reading, in order to write; a man will turn over half a library to make one book.

—Samuel Johnson

I go into my library, and all history unrolls before me. I breathe the morning air of the world while the scent of Eden's roses yet lingered in it, while it vibrated only to the world's first brood of nightengales, and to the laugh of Eve. I see the pyramids building; I hear the shoutings of the armies of Alexander.

—Alexander Smith

He that loves reading has everything within his reach.

—William Godwin

Reading furnishes the mind only with materials of knowledge; it is thinking that makes what we read ours. So far as we apprehend and see the connection of ideas, so far it is ours; without that it is so much loose matter floating in our brains.

—John Locke

Intention, Attention, and Retention

Reading, without some sort of a purpose, is demoralizing. We read for recreation, but thoughtless reading without any purpose, except that of a means of intellectual dissipation, is always demoralizing. It brings on a form of ennui, and makes one restless and discontented instead of happy and contented. To read profitably one must keep these three things in mind: intention, attention, and retention. It is worth noting that the word retention comes from the Latin retces, a net. Nets are made so that the smaller and worthless fishes may slip through the meshes. So the mind trained to retention allows trivial things to escape and holds in memory only things of greater importance.

If you are anxious to improve yourself, read books which tend to elevate your taste, refine your imagination, clarify your ambition, raise your ideals.

Read books of power, books which stir the very depths of your being to some purpose. Read books which make you resolve to do and be a little better; to try a little harder to be somebody and to do something in the world. Fifteen minutes' concentrated reading every day would carry one through the great authors in about five years.

—Dr. Orison S. Marden

C. S. Lewis and the Christian Classics

I myself was first led into reading the Christian classics, almost accidentally, as a result of my English studies. Some, such as Hooker, Herbert, Traherne, Taylor and Bunyan, I read because they are themselves great English writers; others, such as Boethius, St. Augustine, Thomas Aquinas and Dante, because they were "influences". George MacDonald I had found for myself at the age of sixteen and never wavered in my allegiance, though I tried for a long time to ignore his Christianity. They are, you will note, a mixed bag, representative of many Churches, climates and ages. And that brings me to yet another reason for reading them. The divisions of Christendom are undeniable and are by some of these writers most fiercely expressed. But if any man is tempted to think – as one might be tempted who read only contemporaries – that "Christianity" is a word of so many meanings that it means nothing at all, he can learn beyond all doubt, by stepping out of his own century, that this is not so. Measured against the ages "mere Christianity" turns out to be no insipid interdenominational transparency, but something positive, self-consistent, and inexhaustible. I know it, indeed, to my cost. In the days when I still hated Christianity, I learned to recognize, like some all too familiar smell, that almost unvarying *something* which met me, now in Puritan Bunyan, now in Anglican Hooker, now in Thomas Dante. It was there (honeyed and floral) in Francois de Sales; it was there (grave and homely) in Spenser and Walton; it was there (grim but manful) in Pascal and Johnson; there again, with a mild, frightening, Paradisial flavour, in Vaughan and Boehme.

– *God in the Dock*, 1970

Moffat and the Classics

I am not of those who would undervalue any branch of study – they are all valuable. It has been common of late, with certain popular educators, to decry the classics as useless. I cannot agree with them. Classical culture I hold to be of the utmost importance. Language is the medium by which thought is conveyed, and the greater our knowledge of language, the greater our power not only to fully and clearly express our own ideas, but to comprehend with exactness and precision the thoughts of others. Composed as our language is, largely from the Greek, the Latin and the French, some knowledge of these languages is almost a necessity to a proper and ready understanding of our own. I do not say that we may not accomplish much, for we may even acquire excellence in the use of English without a knowledge of the classics. We may, by constant use and reading the best authors after a time become familiar with the meaning of nearly every word in common use; but I do say that it takes as much, if not more time, to master the language in this way than by going direct to the source, and by understanding its derivations, know at once the meaning of a word without referring to a dictionary.

          – from a lecture by John Moffat, 1877

Thoughts About Reading

Reading is the loom on which one's inner garments are woven. Shoddy reading clothes both mind and heart in shoddy garments.

—A. P. Gouthey

There is a certain art in reading. Passive reading is of very little use. We must try to realize what we read. Everybody thinks they know how to read and write; whereas very few people write well, or really know how to read. It is not enough to run our eyes listlessly or mechanically along the lines and turn over the leaves; we must endeavor to realize the scenes described, and the persons who are mentioned, to picture them in the "Gallery of the Imagination."

—John Lubbock

Resolve to edge in a little reading every day, if it is but a single sentence. If you gain fifteen minutes a day, it will make itself felt at the end of the year.

—Horace Mann

Through the years, I have often been asked, at conferences and at other gatherings, "How do you get so much reading done?" May I say here, again, that there is only one way to get any reading done, and that is to read. Whatever reading I may do, I do not deprive myself of needed sleep, and am always in bed for at least eight hours every night; I do not withdraw myself from society; and I am not a man free from obligations, that is, I have been a minister or professor all my adult life, and thus many hours of the day are not my own. There is only one way to get any reading done, and that is to read. If one does not wish to read, he will not read—but if he does not, his ministry will be impoverished indeed.

—Wilbur Smith

Bibliography

BIBLIOGRAPHY
of Recommended Books Currently in Print

Adler, Mortimer. *Aristotle for Everyone.* Macmillan, 1978.

A'Kempis, Thomas. *Imitation of Christ.* Moody Press.

Alexander, A. L. *Poems That Touch the Heart.* Doubleday, 1956.

Allen, James. *As a Man Thinketh.* Executive Books, 1984.

Appleton, Victor. *Tom Swift.* Wanderer Books.

Aurelius, Marcus. *Meditations of.* Harvard University Press.

Bate, W. Jackson. *Samuel Johnson.* Harcourt Brace Jovanovich, 1979.

Beecher, Willard and Marguerite. *Beyond Success and Failure.* Julian Press, 1966.

Bennett, Lerone Jr. *Before the Mayflower: A History of Black America.* Johnson Publishing, 1982.

Bettger, Frank. *How I Raised Myself from Failure to Success in Selling.* Cornerstone, 1975.

Blanchard, Kenneth & Johnson, Spencer. *The One Minute Manager.* Berkley, 1983.

Boorstin, Daniel. *The Discoverers.* Random House, 1983.

Boswell, James. *Life of Johnson.* Penguin, 1979.

Bower, Marvin. *The Will to Manage.* McGraw-Hill, 1966.

Brown, Anthony. *Bodyguard of Lies.* Bantam, 1976.

Burke, Edmund, R

Burnham, John. *Suicide of the West.* John Day, 1964.

Butler A. *Lives of the Saints.* Christian Classics 1962.

Carnegie, Dale. *How to Develop Self Confidence & Influence People By Public Speaking.* Pocket Books, 1977.

Carnegie, Dale. *How to Win Friends & Influence People.* Pocket Books, 1982.

Chambers, Whittaker. *Witness.* Random House, 1952.

Churchill, Winston. *Memoirs of the 2nd World War.* Houghton Mifflin, 1959.

Clark, Leonard. *The Rivers Ran East.* Funk & Wagnalls.

Clason, George. *The Richest Man in Babylon.* Dutton.

Colson, Charles. *Loving God.* Zondervan, 1983.

Conrad, Joseph. *Great Short Works.* Harper & Row.

Conrad, Joseph. *Victory.* Doubleday, 1957.

Costain, Thomas. *The Silver Chalice.* Doubleday, 1954.

Cousin, Norman. *Healing and Belief*. Mosaic Press, 1982.
Cowles, Virginia. *The Great Marlborough and His Duchess*. Macmillan, 1983.
Danco, Leon. *Beyond Survival*. University Press, 1975.
Danforth, William. *I Dare You*. I Dare You Committee, 1976.
de Saint Exupery, Antoine. *The Little Prince*. Harcourt Brace Jovanovich, 1968.
DeHaan, Dan. *The God You Can Know*. Moody Press, 1982.
Dostoyevsky Fyodor. *The Brothers Karamazov*. W. W. Norton, 1976.
Douglass, Lloyd. *Magnificent Obsession*. Houghton Mifflin. 1938.
Doyle, Arthur Conan. *Casebook of Sherlock Holmes*. Berkley, 1982.
Dreiser, Theodore. *The Genius*. Lightyear Press, 1980.
Drucker, Peter. *The Effective Executive*. Harper & Row, 1967.
Drucker, Peter. *The Practice of Management*. Harper & Row, 1954.
Durant, Will. *Story of Philosophy*. Simon & Schuster, 1961.
Durant, Will & Ariel. *Lessons of History*. Simon & Schuster, 1968.
Eliot, George. *Middlemarch*. New American Library.
Emery, Stewart. *Actualization*. Doubleday, 1978.
Evely, Louis. *That Man Is You*. Paulist Press, 1964.
Fisher, Roger & Ury, William. *Getting to Yes*. Houghton Mifflin, 1981.
Flood, Charles. *Lee, The Last Years*. Houghton Mifflin, 1981.
Forester, C. S. *Ship of the Line*. Pinnacle, 1980.
Foster, Richard. *Celebration of Discipline*. Harper & Row, 1978.
Frankl, Victor. *Man's Search for Meaning*. Pocket Books, 1980.
Franklin, Benjamin. *Autobiography*. Random House, 1981.
Fuller, J. F. C. *Grant and Lee*. Indiana Press.
Garnett, David. *Letters of T. E. Lawrence*. CAPE Press, 1933.
Gibbon, Edward. *Decline and Fall of the Roman Empire*. Biblio Distribution Centre, 1978.
Gibran, Kahlil. *The Prophet*. Knopf.
Goble, Frank. *Excellence in Leadership*. Caroline House, 1972.
Grant, James. *Bernard Baruch: The Adventures of a Wall Street Legend*. Simon & Schuster, 1983.

Griswold, A. Whitney. *Liberal Education & the Democratic Ideal*. Greenwood Press, 1976.

Haggai, John. *How to Win Over Worry*, Zondervan.

Haley, Alex. *Roots*. Dell.

Halliburton, Richard. *Royal Road to Romance*. Greenwood Press.

Hamilton, Alexander, et al. *Federalist Papers*. NAL, 1961.

Hamilton, J. Wallace. *Ride the Wild Horses*. Abingdon, 1980.

Hart, Hornell. *Autoconditioning: The New Way to a Successful Life*. Prentice-Hall, 1956.

Hawley, Richard. *The Headmaster's Papers*. Eriksson, 1983.

Hawkins, Norvel. *The Selling Process*.

Hayek, Friedrich. *Road To Serfdom*. Univ. of Chicago, 1944.

Hill, Napoleon. *Think and Grow Rich*. Fawcett, 1979.

Hilton, Conrad. *Be My Guest*. Warner Books, 1983.

Hoffer, Eric. *The True Believer*. Harper & Row.

Homer, *Odyssey*. Harvard University Press.

Hugo, Victor. *Les Miserables*. Modern Library.

Hummel, Charles. *Tyranny of the Urgent*. Inter-Varsity.

Hurnard, Hannah. *Hind's Feet on High Places*. Tyndale, 1979.

Iacocca, Lee. *Iacocca, An Autobiography*. Bantam, 1984.

Jewell, Geri. *Geri*. Ballantine.

Johnson, Dave. *The Success Principle*. Harvest House, 1980.

Johnson, Paul. *Modern Times*. Harper & Row, 1983.

Johnson, Spencer. *One Minute Father*. Morrow, 1983.

Johnson, Spencer. *The Precious Present*.

Jones, Charles. *Life Is Tremendous*. Tyndale, 1981.

Kazantzakis, Nikos. *Last Temptation of Christ*. Simon & Schuster, 1966.

Keller, James. *You Can Change the World*. Halcyon, 1948.

Kennedy, John. *Profiles in Courage*. Harper & Row, 1964.

Ketchum, Richard. *Will Rogers, The Man and His Times*. McGraw-Hill, 1973.

La Rochefoucald, Francois de. *Reflexions ou Sentences et Maximes Morales*. French & European, 1967.

Lasswell, Harold. *Politics: Who Gets What, When & How*. Peter Smith Publisher.

Law, William. *A Serious Call to a Holy Life*. Westminster, 1968.

Lawrence, T. E. *Seven Pillars of Wisdom*. Penguin, 1976.

Levinson, Daniel. *Seasons of a Man's Life*. Knopf, 1978.

Lewis, C. S. *Mere Christianity*. Macmillan, 1978.
Lewis, C. S. *Surprised by Joy*. Harcourt Brace, 1966.
Lindsey, Hall. *Nineteen Eighties Countdown to Armageddon*. Bantam, 1982.
Lockridge, Ross. *Raintree County*. Houghton Mifflin.
Lytle, Clyde. *Leaves of Gold*. Brownlow.
MacArthur, Douglas. *Reminiscences*.
MacDonald, George. *Creation in Christ*. Shaw Pub. 1976.
Maltz, Maxwell. *Psycho-Cybernetics*. Pocket Books.
Manchester, William. *American Caesar*. Dell, 1982.
Manchester, William. *Goodbye, Darkness*. Dell.
Manchester, William. *The Last Lion*. Little Brown, 1983.
Mandino, Og. *The Greatest Miracle in the World*. Bantam, 1977.
Mandino, Og. *The Greatest Salesman in the World*. Bantam, 1978.
Mandino, Og. *The Greatest Success in the World*. Bantam, 1982.
Marshall, Catherine. *A Man Called Peter*. Avon Pub., 1971.
Marshall, Catherine. *Something More*. Revell, 1976.
Marshall & Manuel. *Light & the Glory*. Revell, 1981.
McGrath, William. *The Heart Does Not Speak English*. O'Sullivan Woodside & Co.
Melvill, Herman. *Moby Dick*. Biblio Distribution, 1977.
Miller, Merle. *Plain Speaking*. Berkley, 1982.
Montaigne, Michel de. *Essays*. Biblio Distribution, 1976.
Moorehead, Alan. *The White Nile*. Random House, 1983.
Morgan, Lord. *Churchill Taken from the Diaries of Lord Morgan*. Norman S. Berg, 1976.
Myer, F. W. H. *Human Personality*. Ayer co. 1975.
Naisbitt, John. *Megatrends*. Warner, 1982.
Ogilvie, Lloyd. *Autobiography of God*. Regal Books, 1981.
O'Neill, Eugene. *The Hairy Ape*. Random House, 1973.
Packard, Vance. *Hidden Persuaders*. Pocket Books, 1981.
Paine, Thomas. *Common Sense*. Penguin, 1982.
Peck, M. Scott. *The Road Less Traveled*. Simon & Schuster, 1980.
Peale, Norman Vincent. *The Power of Positive Thinking*. Fawcett, 1978.
Peale, Norman Vincent. *Enthusiasm Makes the Difference*. Fawcett, 1978.

Peters, Thomas & Waterman, Robert. *In Search of Excellence.* Warner, 1983.

Peterson, J. Allan. *Myth of the Greener Grass.* Tyndale House, 1983.

Plato. *The Republic.* Modern Library, 1982.

Powell, John. *Why Am I Afraid to Tell You Who I Am?* Hazelden Foundation.

Rand, Ayn. *Atlas Shrugged.* Random House, 1957.

Rand, Ayn. *The Fountainhead.* NAL.

Robertson, Pat. *The Secret Kingdom.* Thomas Nelson, 1982.

Rogers, Carl. *On Becoming a Person.* Houghton Mifflin, 1961.

Roget, Peter Mark. *Roget's Thesaurus of Synonyms & Antonyms.* Borden.

Royko, Mike. *Boss.* New American Library, 1971.

Sabatini, Rafael. *Scaramouche.* HM.

Sadat, Anwar. *In Search of Identity.* Harper & Row, 1978.

Sandburg, Carl. *Abraham Lincoln.* Harcourt Brace.

Santayana, George. *The Last Puritan.* Charles Scribner's Sons, 1936.

Sayings of the Fathers. Eastern Orthodox, 1975.

Schaeffer, Francis. *How Should We Then Live?* Good News, 1976.

Schell, Jonathan. *The Fate of the Earth.* Avon, 1982.

Schuller, Robert. *Living Positively One Day at a Time.* Fleming H. Revell, 1981.

Schuller, Robert. *Move Ahead With Possibility Thinking.* Jove, 1973.

Schuller, Robert. *Tough Minded Faith for Tender Hearted People.* Thomas Nelson, 1983.

Schuller, Robert. *Tough Times Never Last, But Tough People Do.* Thomas Nelson, 1983.

Schwartz, David. *The Magic of Thinking Big.* Cornerstone, 1962.

Sheehy, Gail. *Passages.* Bantam, 1977.

Solzhenitsyn, Alexander. *The Gulag Archipelago.* Harper & Row, 1974.

Sproul, R. C. *Stronger Than Steel.* Harper & Row, 1983.

Steffens, Lincoln. *Autobiography of Lincoln Steffens.* Harcourt Brace, 1968.

Stern, Aaron. *Me: The Narcissistic American.* Ballantine, 1979.

Stone, W. Clement. *The Success System That Never Fails.* Prentice-Hall, 1962.

Stonecypher, D. D. Jr. *Getting Older and Staying Younger.* Norton, 1980.

Strunk, William Jr. & White, E. B. *Elements of Style.* Macmillan, 1979.

Sumner, William. *Folkways.* Schocken, 1979.

Swindoll, Charles. *Dropping Your Guard.* Word Books.

Swindoll, Charles. *Growing Strong in the Seasons of Life.* Multnomah, 1983.

Swindoll, Charles. *Hand Me Another Brick.* Thomas Nelson, 1978.

Swindoll, Charles. *Three Steps Forward, Two Steps Backward.* Thomas Nelson, 1980.

Thornton, Andre. *Triumph Born of Tragedy.* Harvest House, 1984.

Thornton, John. Believed to be Alive. Eriksson, 1981.

Thucydides. *The Peloponnesian War.* Penguin, 1954.

Tolstoy, Leo. *War and Peace.* Modern Library, 1931.

Tozer, A. W. *Knowledge of the Holy.* Harper & Row, 1978.

Tozer, A. W. *The Pursuit of God.* Tyndale, 1977.

Tuchman, Barbara. *The Guns of August.* Macmillan, 1962.

Tuchman, Barbara. *The March of Folly.* 1984.

Twain, Mark. *Adventures of Tom Sawyer.* Penguin, 1983.

Uris, Leon. *Battle Cry.* Bantam.

Uris, Leon. *Exodus.* Bantam, 1981.

Von Hayek, Friedrich. *Road To Serfdom.* Univ. of Chicago Press, 1944.

Walger, Michael. *Just and Unjust Ways.* Basic Books, 1977.

Wanniski, Jude. *The Way the World Works.* Touchstone, 1983.

Watson, Thomas. *A Business and Its Beliefs.* IBM.

Wheat, Ed. *Love Life for Every Married Couple.* Zondervan, 1980.

Wilbur, William. *Making of George Washington.* Patriotic Education, 1974.

Wilkins & Dunn. *The Real Race.* Tyndale House, 1985.

Williamson, Porter. *Patton's Principles.* Touchstone, 1979.

Wolfe, Tom. *The Right Stuff.* Bantam, 1980.

Wolpe, John. *Our Useless Fears.* Houghton Mifflin, 1981.

268 / People You Meet

Books I've Enjoyed

1.

2.

3.

4.

5.

6.

7.

8.

9.

10.

This list will be enjoyed by you as you review and add to it. It will be cherished by your family as they discover the books that influenced your life.

Books I've Enjoyed

1.

2.

3.

4.

5.

6.

7.

8.

9.

10.

After you complete your list share it with your family, friends and associates

Books I Will Read

1.

2.

3.

4.

5.

6.

7.

8.

9.

10.

Set a reading goal.

Books I Will Read

1.

2.

3.

4.

5.

6.

7.

8.

9.

10.

Biography is the most universally pleasant, universally profitable, of all reading.

— Carlyle

Great Thoughts From Books

1.

2.

3.

4.

5.

6.

7.

8.

9.

10.

Reading without thinking is worse than no reading at all.

—Harry Golden

Great Thoughts From Books

1.

2.

3.

4.

5.

6.

7.

8.

9.

10.

The real purpose of books is to trap the mind into doing its own thinking.

—Christopher Morley

Sharing & Giving

One cardinal rule to remember in reading inspirational books: "You only get to keep and enjoy what you share and give away." If you aren't going to read with the purpose of sharing and giving, I suggest you give the book to someone who will share with you and you'll discover the power of books as you watch your friends grow through sharing with you. Perhaps the best idea would be to use the brain trust idea of *Think and Grow Rich* and both of you begin reading and sharing with each other. (You'd be surprised what could happen in your home life if you tried it there, too.)

—Charles "T" Jones

For additional reading lists or children's reading contracts send stamped self addressed envelope to:

Life Management Services, Inc.
Box 1044
Harrisburg, PA 17108
717-763-1950

I love such books as are either easy and entertaining, and that tickle my fancy, or such as give me comfort, and offer counsel in reordering my life and death.

— Montaigne

My early and invincible love of reading, . . . I would not exchange for the treasures of India.

— Edward Gibbon

If a book comes from the heart, it will contrive to reach other hearts; all art and authorcraft are of small amount to that.

— Carlyle

Every reader reads himself out of the book that he reads; nay, has he a strong mind, reads himself into the book, and amalgamates his thoughts with the author's.

— Goethe

If the crowns of all the kingdoms of Europe were laid down at my feet in exchange for my books and my love of reading, I would spurn them all.

— Fénelon

"A drop of ink may make a million think."   — Byron

They that have read about everything are thought to understand everything too; but it is not always so. Reading furnishes the mind only with the materials of knowledge; it is thinking that makes what we read ours. We are of the ruminating kind, and it is not enough to cram ourselves with a great load of collections, — we must chew them over again.

— Channing